LINDA FERRARI

THE BIG SCORE

GETTING IT & KEEPING IT

BUYING POWER FOR LIFE

Published By:

consumer*power*press

1048 Irvine Avenue, #636
Newport Beach, CA 92660
www.consumerpowerpress.com

Consumer Power Press offers quantity discounts for bulk purchases.
For information, please visit www.consumerpowerpress.com
or call 1-866-541-2500

Printed in the United States of America

ISBN: 978-0-615-22860-0

Library of Congress Cataloging-in-Publication Data

Editor: *Mary Brunson*
Book Design: *Jack Hillman, Hillman Design Group*
Cover Design: *Bill Greaves, Concept West*
Proofreaders: *RK Edit & Exact Dialogue*
Book Production: *Sharon Tully, The Book Producer*
Cover Photography: *Bradford Rogne*

Contents

19 Mortgage & Credit Can't Refinance It, Can't Sell It, and Can't Afford It.. 213

20 Divorce & Credit He Said – She Said What About What The Judge Said?... 225

Dedication

To my daughter Taylor, thank you for your uncompromising love, faith and support during the many years that I have been working on this project. You are a rare gift. To my parents, Barry and Marie, and my brother Tony, thank you for believing in my message and my goals. It has been a long and telling journey.

To my referral partners and the many individuals whose lives and trying times have contributed to the endless research and case studies that have given me the knowledge and expertise to write this book, thank you and stay on course!

To my editor, Mary Brunson, I could not have done it without you.

And finally, thank you to all of my very close friends who have stood by me and inspired me when I had to stay home and write instead of sharing a great bottle of red with you!

Introduction

Over the past decade our credit scores have been revealed to us, but little else has been shared with us about them. That's a big problem because those 3-digit numbers are, de facto, the biggest obstacles for more than 228 million Americans. And it's only getting worse.

The U.S. economy depends heavily on the emotional and financial strength of American consumers. A whopping 66% of the U.S. economic engine is powered by the willingness of every American to commit his or her hard-earned assets to buy the goods and services that will benefit one's family. They do so because they possess the confidence that their jobs, their homes, and their economic futures will not suffer as a result. But consumers are uncertain, and they are worried more than ever before.

Continued bad news about the mortgage crisis draws in new victims and homeowners wonder if the unthinkable–foreclosure–will happen to them. And it doesn't stop there. A hostile lending environment finds Americans questioning how they can stay afloat in a system they don't understand. Worse, many are too frightened to ask the right questions, or don't even know what the "right" questions are.

Convinced that reviewing one's credit report will bring more frustration than stepping onto the bathroom scale the day after Thanksgiving, many people simply ignore their credit until that inevitable day when they face a pressing need or desire to make a purchase that requires good credit scores.

Why? People are hindered by the fact that they never learned anything about credit. It's not part of the educational curriculum, and usually not a topic parents discuss with their children. When your parents sat you down for an important talk, did they ever say, "I want to talk to you about your credit scores"? I don't think so. Everything you have learned about credit has come from the school of hard knocks.

The linchpin issue right now and for the coming decade is **credit.** Good news? High scores are the golden ticket for financial freedom. Bad news? Low credit scores will impair your abilities to function in today's society. Low credit scores make it difficult to get insurance, an apartment, a cell phone, a car, a job, and this problem is only going to become more invasive as time passes.

I am a credit improvement and education expert. I've helped thousands conquer their credit challenges. Among those who have come to me for assistance are Hollywood celebrities, prominent sports figures, successful business executives, regular families struggling to pay their bills, victims of identity theft, people facing bankruptcy, and those with mortgage challenges.

Some come to me seeking to raise their credit scores from a 720 to a 780. Others need to recover from a severe financial crisis. Whatever the reason, all share the same problem–they do not understand their credit or how the credit scoring system works. In fact, most people who have high credit scores are completely clueless as to how they achieved that standard. That's where their potential problems rest. They become incredibly vulnerable to an instant, devastating drop in their scores. A credit score of 750 can drop to a 620 in less than a minute. And on the other side, most who have low scores are misguided as to why their scores are low.

This book seeks to change that.

The scoring system as it stands today has many flaws. But it's the only system we have. My ultimate goal is to use my experience to help develop legislation that will fully protect consumers. However, the wheels of bureaucracy turn slowly, and people need help now; the type of help found in this book. It explains how to make the system work for you; not against you.

At times it might seem that my advice runs counter to the traditionally accepted remedies, i.e., not paying collections or disputing accounts that the credit card holder would otherwise hesitate to question. I'm not suggesting defiance without a cause. Nor am I recommending that people try to avoid paying a legitimate debt. My sole point is that because flaws occur in the credit scoring system, as in any other business, consumers must thoroughly examine their charges and the consequences of their actions in handling credit conflicts. Although (as you will learn by reading this book) the majority of discrepancies are *not* consumer driven, keep in mind that the burden falls on the consumer, you, to prove the error and to fight until it's rectified.

I love what I do and I am passionate about sharing my knowledge to empower you and help improve your financial outlook. When you have a clear picture of how the credit scoring system works, you will no longer be held captive by your creditors. You will receive offers that are available to only the most credit-worthy individuals, and rather than struggle to keep up, you will be able to direct your financial future. The Big Score makes it possible.

I hope you enjoy reading this book as much as I enjoyed writing it.

CHAPTER 1

Why I Wrote This Book

There are thousands of books that tell you how to make a budget you can actually stick to, or how you can better manage your debt or avoid financial disaster by spending more wisely. When I went in search of a user-friendly, straight-talk book about credit scoring, one written by a credit expert with actual hands-on experience who really understands the inner workings of the credit system, I was stunned to come up completely empty handed. I instantly realized that it was my mission to deliver this book: an expert's how-to-guide for getting and keeping good credit.

I wrote this book for you. I wrote it because I know you have dreams of providing for your family, living better, and retiring comfortably someday. I wrote this book because I know you need and deserve to live a life that will let you sleep and breathe better. I wrote it because I know credit concerns erode spirits, diminish life's simple joys, and deprive each and everyone who suffers these difficulties from being the person he or she was born to be. I understand your worries, and I understand the system.

The credit problems you read about are not only scary; they're very real. Yet the fixes suggested by politicians seem conjured out of pure fantasy. I don't understand how, on the one hand, our nation's leaders can imply that the solution to the nation's bad credit problem is to simply stop giving credit to people with low scores and to charge people with low scores more money for credit. And on the other hand, bail out the corporations whose products are the root of the economic problems we face time and time again nation-wide. Credit-weary individuals do not need to be punished. They need to be educated about the credit scoring system, and this book does just that.

We are forced to manage the most important financial element of our lives, one which directly impacts our nation's overall economic health, and to do so without any type of training. Our schools teach us about history, grammar, and foreign language, all very important subjects, yet I don't recall being taught how to manage my credit, do you? And regardless of what you read and hear, there's a lot more to calculating that 3-digit number than paying your bills on time. I advocate that an 8-hour course on Credit Management be a prerequisite to graduating high school. Wouldn't that be a great start to empowering the next generation with the knowledge to control and manage their own financial destiny!

From my expert perspective, there are three areas in critical need of immediate attention: *The Lack of Education*, as just noted; *The Vagueness of the Laws Intended to Protect Us;* and, *Consumer Credit Rights & The Constitution.*

Yes, there are ACTS in place intended to protect us, but most of this legislation is vague and open ended. Loopholes in the laws make them very difficult to enforce (more on this in Chapter 2.) Worse, even if the consumer can make a clear case with current legislation, most cannot afford to fight against the multi-billion dollar companies who have lawyers on the payroll to fight credit cases all day, everyday. Can you win? Maybe. Can you afford to lose? Highly doubtful. So consumers largely forfeit their rights because they can't afford the case.

Make no mistake, when it comes to credit, consumers are guilty until proven innocent. We all realize this premise flies in the face of the Fifth Amendment of the U.S. Constitution which states, in part, "No person shall be ... deprived of life, liberty, or property without due process of law." According to the rights our forefathers fought for, you cannot be executed, imprisoned, or fined without the proper course of justice taking place—a fair trial. The burden of proof should be on the prosecution, which must collect and present substantial evidence to convince the judge and jury that the accused is guilty beyond a reasonable doubt. In case of remaining doubts, the accused is to be acquitted.

It may sound a little extreme to invoke the Constitution, but is it really? Credit scores can give or take a form of freedom that will determine whether or not you're going to live the American dream. That means buying a home, sending your kids to college, or starting a business.

If you've ever tried to work with the credit bureaus to have inaccurate information removed or updated on your credit reports, I think you'll agree that it can be one of the most frustrating experiences you will ever have. So much so that it's one of the reasons many don't even bother checking their credit. The credit bureaus will tell you to contact the creditor. The creditor will tell you they have sold the account. The four collection agencies the accounts have now been sold to will not respond to your certified request for proof of their claim. So how—if you couldn't get verification from the creditor or collection agency—can the credit bureaus say that the account has been verified and that any further request for investigation will be considered frivolous? So, without even understanding what happened, most consumers just acquiesce. And in doing so they doom themselves to collectively spending billions more a year on higher interest rates, penalty fees, and late fees, all because of low credit scores calculated on inaccurate information.

I've seen thousands of people pay debts that did not even belong to them because they were afraid of having their wages garnished, or their homes taken away. I have seen hundreds of people go through bankruptcy because they didn't know they had any other option and were afraid of confronting their creditors to ask for help or consideration.

So why did I write this book? Because it includes interesting and *crucially important* information that you, as a consumer and an empowered member of society, should have. And to say that you need it, that's putting it mildly! My desire is that when you've finished reading this book you'll be able to clearly and fearlessly, look at your 3-digit credit scores and know that you–not your creditors and not the credit bureaus–hold the key to your financial success and the American dream.

CHAPTER 2

The Flaws You Need
To Know To Survive

Every system has its flaws. Sometimes you have to dig to find them, and sometimes they slap you in the face. Every day more and more consumers take serious, costly hits because of flaws within the credit scoring system. I'm convinced the flaws will keep increasing until consumers reach a boiling point. Once they've had enough, they'll be forced to take action—to get involved.

Yet it's important to remember that the current scoring system was developed in the 1950s. Think about that. This system was in place a decade before astronaut Neil Armstrong set foot on the moon. The television sitcom "Leave It to Beaver" hadn't been aired. Singer Elvis Presley was just beginning to make young girls swoon.

If you consider the antiquated system at work, you can begin to understand why problems exist. Credit scoring is always behind the times. The extent of the problem becomes even more apparent when you realize that, until 2004, credit reports and scores were more or less inaccessible to consumers. Without access to those scores and reports, people were helpless. They lacked the ability to question the system. They could not request changes or demand improvements to their scores. They were at the mercy of the credit bureaus and creditors.

My purpose is not to condemn the only system available. Part of my role as a credit expert is to reveal the flaws of the credit system and fight to implement changes. Being realistic, I don't expect change overnight. I could spend my time carrying a picket sign in front of the United States Capitol building to support changes that reflect the times and the needs of today's consumers. Or, I can reach out to consumers directly, making them aware of the flaws so they can make the system work in their favor. I choose the latter. The promise by credit industry leaders or legislators of a watered-down compromise initiative six years down the road means nothing to people whose problems exist now.

Consider that the key to successfully managing credit aimed at getting and keeping The Big Score rests not in doing the *right thing* from an ethical standpoint, but in doing the *right thing* from a legally strategic standpoint. The only way to accomplish that goal is to recognize that sometimes the appropriate action is one that seems counterintuitive. That's where understanding flaws in the credit scoring system pays off.

The Flaws

Guilty Until Proven Innocent

Yes, it runs counter to the essence of the U.S. Constitution; but in the eyes of industry professionals who implement the credit scoring system you are guilty until proven innocent–the burden of proof falls on you. If you fail to convince these professionals that you are not at fault, you will be held accountable. And sometimes, even if you prove your case, getting the creditors and credit bureaus to alter their records is virtually impossible without filing a lawsuit.

This system doesn't favor the consumer. Case in point, consumers must produce actual documents to have inaccuracies removed from their credit files, while those furnishing the credit information only have to send a tape-to-disc transfer. This is unreasonable. When creditors first supply a derogatory report about you to the credit bureaus, they are not required to provide documents, proof of signature, or proof of actual ownership of their claim. Yet it is only after the damage has been done that consumers can challenge the accuracy of accounts.

One simple error on their part, a number transposition, clicking on the wrong box and BAM! Your score can plummet 100 points. Unless you can afford to hire a savvy attorney, it takes months, sometimes years, to prove your case. Face it, if you pit most consumer bank accounts against the credit bureaus, there is no doubt who will prevail.

It's not right. People with their credit challenges should be *innocent until proven guilty*, just as they are in our legal system.

Their Mistake, Your Loss – Credit Reporting Errors

The subprime mortgage crisis fallout which began in December 2006 has thrust the issue of credit into the political spotlight. Lenders provided financing to hundreds of thousands of homeowners who—based on the terms of their agreements—could not realistically pay back their loans.

During one of the many 2008 political news conferences and debates, candidates were talking about the fact that millions who potentially faced foreclosure could not refinance at a better interest rate to save their homes because their credit scores are too low. When asked to weigh in, chills went up my spine when I heard one of the candidates suggest, more or less, that the solution to the crisis would be to stop giving credit to people who do not have good credit.

That would be a reasonable option if there was any guarantee that consumer credit scores were always correct. But in reality, that's far from the case. And statistics will show you that most mistakes are NOT consumer driven.

The U.S. Public Interest Research Groups (USPIRGs), conducted a 30-state study on the subject of credit scoring, and published their own report: *Mistakes Do Happen: A Look at Errors in Consumer Credit Reports*. The study revealed that 79% of consumer credit reports contain errors.[1] What's more, there's a one-in-four chance your credit report contains an error serious enough to cause you to be denied credit. Not good!

Through my credit improvement operations, I've now personally analyzed more than 14,000 credit reports. My company has analyzed thousands more. Why is this important? I can count on one hand those that had zero mistakes! That's important for you to know because statistics indicate that only 79% of credit reports have errors. My vast experience shows otherwise, with as many as 99% having some sort of error–a misspelled name, a wrong address, an incorrect balance on an account, or an inaccurately reported serious derogatory.

The overwhelming presence of errors in credit reports is devastating to consumers because they are the ones who pay for those errors. As you will see throughout this book they pay in various ways, and they pay BIG!

The Secret Formula

Lenders hold consumers to a high standard. They insist that consumers build and maintain credit scores in the 750 area, or else suffer substantial punitive consequences. This is an exceptionally difficult task when consumers don't even know the formula used to calculate those scores. The average individual understands only that he or she is held to a high standard. How can anyone hold consumers accountable for something they don't understand, or for what no one will tell them? Worse yet, the credit reporting agencies are raking in tons of profit by charging consumers for reports containing their own personal information.

What I'd like to see would be for elected officials to unite and pass a bill that gives consumers more access to the secret formula for credit scoring. Not only would that enable everyone to save more for their futures, it might even help mitigate Social Security woes.

It's time for people to gain an understanding of how their scores are calculated.

Creditors Profit From Consumer Lack Of Knowledge

This is a biggie. Again I must emphasize that consumers are held to a high standard of excellence and consistency in their credit history, but they are not provided with the "how to" manual about how to achieve this. Meanwhile, creditors benefit immensely from consumers' lack of knowledge.

According to the latest credit score survey commissioned by the Consumer Federation of America (CFA) in 2008, consumers could save $28 billion a year in lower credit card finance charges if they improved credit scores by 30 points.[2] Let me repeat, that's $28 billion a year!

The survey also found that only one-third of those surveyed even knew what a credit score was, let alone how it impacted their financial well-being. Here's a breakdown:

- 31% understood the meaning of a credit score.

- A mere 47% knew that Experian, Equifax, and TransUnion are the three national credit bureaus.

- 72% believed that with credit scores under 700 they could get a low-cost mortgage.

- 29% thought a 400-500 score would qualify them for a low-cost mortgage.

- Only 45% realized that consumers have more than one score.

- 74% believed that scores were influenced by income (not true).

- 34% believed that the state where they lived and their ethnicity influenced their scores.

These statistics are disturbing enough; yet even these do not reflect my experience. After working with thousands of credit challenged consumers, I find that less than 15% of the individuals I speak with possess a basic understanding of the credit reporting system.

There are many functions in life that people can learn on their own because they are intuitive, like walking or riding a bike. Unfortunately, there's nothing intuitive about the credit scoring system.

Universal Default Should Be A Crime

As discussed above, The Consumer Federation of America estimates that low credit scores–which, as I've noted, are largely the result of credit reporting errors–cost consumers an extra $28 billion a year in additional interest rates and fees on credit cards due to a phenomenon called *Universal Default*. [2] This number is up $8 billion since 2007.

When it comes to your credit, you have to make certain that you manage every aspect of it perfectly, and at all times. Believe it or not, a drop in your credit scores can cause *ALL* of your credit card interest rates to skyrocket. I talk more about this in Chapter 8.

Essentially, universal defaults will spread like a nasty virus throughout every aspect of your credit, causing you to instantly be charged punitive rates for every credit account you have. Outstanding credit card debt in this country is more than $968 billion dollars. [3] An instant and punitive rate increase can prove devastating to consumers who suffer across-the-board increases in their monthly obligations.

Collection Agencies Have Master Power To Destroy Without A Legal Binding Agreement

When you sign an agreement to pay, whether for a credit card account or for an installment loan such as a mortgage or new car, the agreement you are signing is with the original creditor. So why is the *collection agency* allowed to report the item on your credit when you never signed a legal binding agreement to pay them? In most cases, when consumers incur a collection, usually it's because they have a loss of employment, illness, issues with medical insurance not paying, or simply because they lack the ability to pay—they've done nothing illegal. By contrast, collection agencies break the law ALL THE TIME. It's an incredible flaw in the system. Yet, without any legal binding agreement, collection agencies have the master power to destroy your credit.

One Free Credit Report Per Year – Big Deal!

The Fair and Accurate Credit Transactions Act of 2003, an amendment to the Fair Credit Reporting Act (both of which I will talk about in Chapter 13), allows consumers to request and obtain a free credit report once every 12 months from each of the three major credit bureaus, Equifax, Experian, and TransUnion.

Here's the flaw. It took more than forty years for consumers to get free and easy access to one's own credit reports. I don't want to burst anyone's bubble, but today a credit report without a credit score means nothing. Everyone who wants his or her scores must pay a fee at the time of ordering one's free report. Since it's the scores that are the number one decision factor in lending, shouldn't these also be free at least once every 12 months?

Too Many Scores To Manage

You know what they say about too many cooks spoiling the broth. That's nothing compared to too many considerations killing credit scores. As if the multiple factors that make up your credit scores from various credit reporting agencies were not enough to keep heads spinning, every consumer has different scores for different borrowing purposes. These include consumer credit scores, auto loan scores, insurance scores, and mortgage scores. Wouldn't it make more sense to have ONE score to manage?

CREDIT TIP

Mortgage Scores carry the strictest criteria. Therefore, setting your standards at that level will bolster the chances of getting the highest possible scores in other areas.

Creditors & Credit Bureaus Overrule Our Court System

No doubt about it, few experiences in life are as trying as a divorce. Certainly, every spouse feels total relief when he or she has been awarded a judgment that says you are free from your ex's credit card debt or car loan. Not so fast, though.

Bottom line is that a divorce decree does NOT take precedence over a creditor agreement. In other words, the credit bureaus and creditors actually trump a divorce settlement, making you liable for your spouse's debt *regardless* of what the judge says.

I've have had this conversation a thousand times. It's just too hard to believe, and many of my clients refuse to accept it. However, at least until legislation is amended to address the issue, this one is set in stone. I talk about this more in Chapter 20.

Paying Debt In This System Makes Scores Go Down

Crazy, but true. Paying a collection can actually bring credit scores down. You'd think that making good on your debt would cause credit scores to improve. But, what really happens is that when you pay a collection that's originally more than 12 months old, it becomes a *recent* paid collection on your credit report, after which your credit scores can immediately drop by as much as 100 points.

The Amount of the Derogatory Debt Does Not Matter

A collection is a collection—no matter the dollar figure. The same rule applies to tax liens and judgments. To the scoring system the derogatory amount can be $100 or $100,000, and your credit scores are impacted the same. This seems ludicrous and unjust because many of those small collections result from medical billing errors. Others represent collections that originated from annual fees added to old credit card accounts no longer in use. Don't think a small dollar amount will be any less damaging to your scores. This has all the signs of a blanket judgment which is biased and flawed.

Triple Jeopardy

We've all heard of Double Jeopardy, a procedural defense and *constitutional right* that prohibits a defendant from being tried twice for the same crime on the same set of facts. Well, in the credit scoring system, one derogatory account can be reported up to three times—*Triple Jeopardy*. If the original creditor sells the debt to a collection agency, both the original creditor *and* the collection agency can report the account. Then, if the original creditor or collection agency files a judgment, the public record is also reported. And all these records show the past due debt and all deal serious derogatory penalties to credit scores. The really bad news here? There's NO legislation or regulation whatsoever in the current ACTS to protect you. One way or the other the creditors, collection agencies, courts and credit bureaus are able to do WHATEVER they want—while unwitting consumers are left to deal with Triple Jeopardy.

The Punishment Doesn't Fit The Crime

Most consumers believe that being a little late in paying a bill is merely a symbol of our hectic lifestyle. Surely the creditors and the credit bureaus understand, right? Wrong! Just a single 30-day late pay can lower your score by 80 points. That reality exposes an enormous flaw. After all, a collection causes you to lose approximately 100 points, but the gravity of this is far more severe than a 30-day late. The difference behind the derogatory is huge. So you should not be penalized as much. There should be caps on score penalties which consider the type of derogatory, the amount of derogatory, and the number of derogatories.

Hardship? Deal With It!

There is nothing remotely human about the credit system. This is an especially difficult reality for individuals who find themselves in the midst of a crisis. Everyone has dark times in their lives: illness, a death in the family, job loss, unexpected expenses, etc. When hardship occurs and people cannot keep pace with their bills, they can instantly be labeled as a default. That means they could lose everything that they've worked for. That is just not right.

Even worse, there are no laws in place requiring that creditors report negative information to the credit bureaus. Here's the section of the law from the Fair Credit Reporting Act:

§623. Responsibilities of furnishers of information to consumer reporting agencies [15 U.S.C. § 1681s-2]

(a) Duty of Furnishers of Information to Provide Accurate Information

(7) Negative Information

(E) *Use of notice without submitting negative information.* No provision of this paragraph shall be construed as requiring a financial institution that has provided a customer with a notice described in subparagraph (A) to furnish negative information about the customer to a consumer reporting agency.

Here's the text from subparagraph (A):

(A) *In general.* A person who furnishes information to a consumer reporting agency regarding a delinquent account being placed for collection, charged to profit or loss, or subjected to any similar action shall, not later than 90 days after furnishing the information, notify the agency of the date of delinquency on the account, which shall be the month and year of the commencement of the delinquency on the account that immediately preceded the action.

If I were in a position of authority, I would initiate legislation that allows for hardship cases. If a person shows legitimate proof, then creditors should be required to provide lenience and be disallowed from blacklisting a person's credit standing. There should also be varying levels of hardship. For instance, there should be an established timeframe payment extension for consumers who have lost their jobs, especially due to a sluggish economy.

Don't bother wasting your precious time pouring your heart out to the creditors or credit bureaus. They don't care. They have heard all the sob stories. And they've become immune to people's woes. For them business is business. Maybe that will change. But for now, that's the harsh reality.

The Laws Are Flawed — All Smoke & Mirrors

Following in the footsteps of the Guilty Until Proven Innocent flaw, for every consumer who has ever tried to challenge the accuracy of a derogatory account on his or her credit reports, I know you will agree that this is a big flaw in the system. Basically, when it comes to derogatory information on your credit reports, the law states that you have the right to ask for two things:

1. Verification of the claim from the creditor, court or collection agency reporting it; and

2. For the credit bureaus to investigate the validity of the item with the creditor, court, or collection agency.

If either of these two requests are not responded to under certain guidelines, as follows, then the items must be deleted from your credit reports. But the process DOES NOT WORK for consumers.

This is because the law is unclear and left open to interpretation. There is no concrete language establishing the definition of the terms "reasonable procedures," "reasonable investigation," "verification," or "unverifiable." Stricter guidelines must be put into place to make the investigation and verification procedures clearer and more demanding of the creditors and credit bureaus.

Following are the key sections that pertain to this flaw. You decide. You can access the full content of the Acts on my site, http://www.lindaferrari.com.

Fair Credit Reporting Act (FCRA)

- **§ 607. Compliance procedures [15 U.S.C. § 1681e].** This is the section that regulates how the credit to bureaus report information about consumers to lenders. The following key text from this section proves that consumer protection offered is useless without a term definition for "reasonable procedures."

    "(b) *Accuracy of report.* Whenever a consumer reporting agency prepares a consumer report it shall follow ***reasonable proce-***

dures to assure maximum possible accuracy of the information concerning the individual about whom the report relates."

- **§ 611. Procedure in case of disputed accuracy [15 U.S.C. § 1681i].** This is the section that regulates how the credit bureaus handle investigation of a disputed account. Again, consumer protection offered is useless without a term definition for "reasonable investigation."

    "(1) Reinvestigation Required

    (A) *In general.* Subject to subsection (f), if the completeness or accuracy of any item of information contained in a consumer's file at a consumer reporting agency is disputed by the consumer and the consumer notifies the agency directly, or indirectly through a reseller, of such dispute, the agency shall, free of charge, conduct a ***reasonable reinvestigation*** to determine whether the disputed information is inaccurate and record the current status of the disputed information, or delete the item from the file."

Fair And Accurate Credit Transaction Act (FACTA)

It was finally recognized that the FCRA did not address the verification process in sufficient detail, and thus in 2003 the Fair and Accurate Credit Transaction Act (FACTA) came along as an amendment. Here's the language of FACTA that pertains to this issue:

- **Section 313. FTC And Consumer Reporting Agency Action Concerning Complaints**

    "(A) consumer disputes with consumer reporting agencies over the accuracy or completeness of information in a consumer's file are promptly and fully investigated and any incorrect, incomplete, or ***unverifiable*** information is corrected or deleted immediately thereafter;"

- **Section 314. Improved Disclosure Of The Results Of Reinvestigation.**

    "(i) promptly delete that item of information from the file of the consumer, or modify that item of information, as appropriate, based on the results of the *reinvestigation*; and"

- **Section 314. Improved Disclosure Of The Results Of Reinvestigation.**

"(E) if an item of information disputed by a consumer is found to be inaccurate or incomplete or cannot be *verified* after any *reinvestigation* under paragraph (1), for purposes of reporting to a consumer reporting agency only, as appropriate, based on the results of the reinvestigation promptly—

   (i)   *modify* that item of information;

   (ii)   *delete* that item of information; or

   (iii)   *permanently block the reporting of that item* of information."

- **Section 317. Reasonable Reinvestigation Required.**

"Section 611(a)(1)(A) of the Fair Credit Reporting Act (15 U.S.C. 1681i(a)(1)(A)) is amended by striking "shall reinvestigate free of charge" and inserting "shall, free of charge, conduct a *reasonable reinvestigation* to determine whether the disputed information is inaccurate."

Here's the flaw: The laws don't work! Period. And the legislators responsible for writing and enacting the new laws do not properly regulate the creditors and the credit bureaus. So, in reality, nothing has changed. It's all smoke and mirrors. So, riddle me this: What do you think is the most commonly used and printed phrase employed by all three credit bureaus to respond to consumer disputes?

"We have verified that this item belongs to you."

There has to be a better way!

THE REAL DEAL

The massive creditors and credit bureaus carry enormous influence. Reform is bitterly fought as highly paid credit industry lobbyists maintain their reign over an industry. That explains why the system is so flawed. Industry leaders make enormous sums of money by keeping people in the dark. They know the system is broken, and they refuse to fix it. Why? It comes down to dollars and cents. Meanwhile, consumers endure the nonsense.

The only hope is the politicians. They have the power to do the right thing. The sole benefit of an archaic, senseless system is that no one can honestly argue that it works sufficiently or even qualifies as mediocre. If they examine it thoroughly, without any preconceived notions, they will see a system that manipulates individuals on a grand scale. They will see a system that undermines the American Dream–a system that needs attention now.

[1] http://static.uspirg.org/reports/MistakesDoHappen2004.pdf
[2] http://www.consumerfed.org/pdfs/Credit_Score_PR_7-10-08.pdf
[3] http://www.federalreserve.gov/releases/G19/Current/g19.pdf

CHAPTER 3

Credit Awareness: Out Of The Shadows & Into The Spotlight

During the past few years the significance of credit awareness has gone mainstream. Every time you open up your web browser or a newspaper, or turn on the television, there's another feature, notice or ad highlighting how "you too can have a 780 credit score." I have beaten the drum for years about the importance of credit education, and I am pleased that this important issue has finally moved out of the shadows and into the spotlight where it belongs. But, it can often be difficult to separate good advice from bad advice or even from a well-disguised sales pitch. Remember, if it sounds too good to be true then it probably is!

Not All Credit Repair Advice Is Good!

With years of experience in the trenches of credit repair, I can tell you that most of the information you hear or read about credit is incorrect or misleading. Credit awareness is monumentally important, and reliable information is critical. There are too many self-proclaimed "financial experts" now offering credit improvement tips to consumers even though they have never repaired anyone's credit. This phenomenon should greatly concern you. When you need credit help, you don't have the time to go down a wrong path or be led astray on the advice of someone who has hopped on the bandwagon because credit is now such a popular media topic.

Everyone has his or her strengths. Mine is that I am a full-fledged credit improvement and education expert. I have earned the right to say this because I have helped improve literally thousands of individuals credit scores, enabling them to strengthen their financial outlooks and realize the dreams that strong credit scores support.

I am not saying this to self-promote; I'm simply pointing out the extreme difference between an expert who writes superficially on a vast number of topics, including mortgages, equity investments, insurance, credit and every other finance-related subject versus someone who knows credit inside and out.

WORD OF CAUTION

When reading this book, resist the temptation to "cherry pick" advice that piques your interest or curiosity. You might inadvertently take an item out of context and act on it without understanding how it relates to or impacts other factors. It is essential to read the entire book before deciding on the appropriate course of action for your situation.

How To Separate Good Advice From Bad!

Don't Use Credit Cards—Pay Everything In Cash

Pay Off All Collections Before Applying for A Loan

Close Accounts You Don't Need or Use

Pay Off Your Auto Loan So Your Debt Ratio Goes Down

All sounds like great advice, right? I can tell you first hand that all of these items will negatively impact your credit scores. As you can see, it's not always easy to separate good advice from bad.

Haste definitely makes waste when it comes to making decisions about how to handle credit challenges, and in some cases it is almost impossible to reverse a wrong decision. Taking action on bad advice can cause an instant drop of up to 100 points or more to your credit scores. Trust me on this. In later chapters, I will show you how a drop of 100 points can cost thousands of dollars per month in additional interest rates and fees. That's an attention grabber, isn't it?

Here are some tips to help you separate good advice from bad when it comes to your credit:

- **Get Educated.** Knowing how to separate good advice from bad is not easy, but it can be done if you do your research. You have taken the first step by deciding to read this book, and when finished you'll have a better understanding of how the credit scoring system works than do most professionals who offer credit repair services.

- **Ask for a referral.** Asking for a referral from a source that you can trust is a great step toward separating bad advice from good. In many cases you will find that your realtor, your mortgage professional, your accountant, or your attorney can recommend a trust-worthy credit improvement expert or firm that can answer your questions.

- **Don't Buy Into a Sales Pitch.** Firms that advertise on television or in the newspaper are generally staffed with salespeople, not specialists who can help you. My company has never advertised to the consumer directly. We have always received our business primarily through word of mouth.

- **Expect to Pay.** Don't expect to receive good advice for free. Everyone has to make a living. If you call on a professional credit expert for advice, expect to pay as you would an attorney, or an accountant.

- **Ask Questions.** Make sure the credit specialist you are talking to or taking advice from can tell you how credit scores are calculated. In this book I will talk about many factors involved in calculating a credit score. Without this knowledge, it would be impossible to create a strategy to successfully improve credit scores.

- **Be Realistic.** Improving credit scores takes time. Watch out for companies or individuals promising miracles will occur in a few days or weeks. Remember, it took time for your scores to get where they are, and it will take at least 3-6 months, depending on your challenges, to improve your situation. It can take up to a year or more if you have multiple collections, tax lien, bankruptcy, or identity theft issues.

- **Participate.** One of the reasons my program is so successful is that I require participation from my clients. I load them up with education and I require that they manage their credit in a specific manner. Your participation not only ensures a higher level of success, it ensures a greater knowledge base.

THE REAL DEAL

You can achieve credit improvement success. It's not rocket science. It's knowing your rights and the inner workings of the system. That's precisely why it's essential to know you can trust the person who gives you advice regarding your credit and financial issues. The right person can do great things. The right advice will advance your goals. Conversely, the wrong advice can lead you down a path that runs at odds with your long-term goals.

Regardless of whether you are on the verge of bankruptcy, with a credit score of 550, or whether you have a credit score of 720 and want to achieve and keep a 780, improving your credit scores is completely do-able. Believe me. I have seen it all, and there is very little that can't be improved if you tap into the right resources.

CHAPTER 4

The Cost of NOT Paying Attention

You just learned that credit card companies make an extra $28 billion a year from consumers with low credit scores. But this is merely the tip of the iceberg when it comes to the real cost of low credit scores.

In the past, the credit report was instrumental in determining whether a consumer had the ability to purchase big-ticket items such as homes, cars, and appliances. This is no longer the case. Today your credit report is pulled even when you start a new account for your telephone, electricity and other utilities. And it doesn't stop there, not by a long shot. When your credit scores are low, you pay more for *everything*.

No one has unlimited income, and no one wants to work forever. Every opportunity you have to reduce what you pay for your mortgage, your car, and your credit cards is money you can use to fund your retirement, pay for college education, and use for a brighter future. It's money you can use to establish a more solid financial footing so that you can be more comfortable and worry less.

How Did Consumers Get Here?

Over the past decade, credit reports have moved out of the dark confines of the credit bureaus' filing cabinets and rightfully into the hands of consumers.

That's good news! Now you can see your credit report with the click of a mouse. You can see firsthand the items that are adding to, or dragging down your credit scores. But, there is some bad news that goes with the good; having access to information about your credit report raises the bar on your own accountability. Lenders have a higher expectation, because now you can monitor your credit records and take proactive measures to gain higher scores.

Unfortunately, although credit reports are more accessible than ever, many consumers are turning a blind eye to seeing what's in their report until it's too late and the opportunity is lost.

How Credit Scores Affect Mortgage Payments

FACT

According to a recent survey conducted by the National Association for Business Economics, the combined threat of subprime loan defaults and excessive indebtedness has overtaken terrorism and the Middle East as the biggest short-term threat to the U.S. economy.[1]

This puts all borrowers in a position to substantiate the ability to make payments on their mortgage loans. And a home as collateral is not the golden ticket it once was. Lenders don't want to be property owners. They want to collect on money loaned.

Here's a short list of how much low credit scores can cost when it comes to a mortgage:

1. **You May Never Own A Home AT ALL, AGAIN, Or FOR YEARS**

   Whether or not you've always had poor credit, or have just suffered from the recent mortgage crisis, this is a very real possibility for individuals. If you have low scores or problematic reports, lenders will either deny you flat out or penalize you with such exorbitant rates that the outcome ranges from completely undesirable to impossible.

2. **You Will Pay Higher Interest Rates**

   It just makes sense that if you have higher credit scores, you will pay a lower interest rate on your mortgage loan and will have to put less down. Fair Isaac's consumer website at http://www.myfico.com offers a mortgage payment calculator that is updated regularly to show consumers how their FICO score can affect their interest rate.

Per myfico.com, if your credit scores are under 620, consumers could pay $1420 more per month than someone with a 720 credit score for a 30-Year Fixed Rate Mortgage with a loan principal amount of $300,000. That's an *additional* $17,040 per year, and approximately $511,151 over the life of the loan.

Of course, interest rates are determined by many factors but the bottom line is that individuals with *low credit scores will pay nearly three times more in interest than those with strong credit scores.*

3. **Now You Will Be Subject To Loan Level Price Adjustment Fees (LLPA's) when applying for a conventional mortgage.**

Consumers with a middle score of less than 719 will now be charged an LLPA fee which was implemented by Fannie Mae and Freddie Mac in March of 2008. See the following chart to see where your scores fall [2]:

FICO Score	LLPA You Will Pay
Below 620	2.750%
620-639	2.250%
640-659	1.500%
660-679	1.000%
680-719	0.250%

For people experiencing the worst-case scenario, carrying a middle credit score of less than 620 could cost you an extra $8,250 upfront on a $300,000 loan amount.

4. **You Will Pay More For Private Mortgage Insurance (PMI)**

PMI is insurance that mortgage lenders require from most homebuyers who have less than a 20% down payment on their property. If your credit scores are marginal, your private mortgage insurance rate might be hundreds of dollars higher per month than you expect, and you usually don't find this out until closing.

5. **You Will Compromise Your Ability To Refinance For "Cash Out"**

As you build equity in the ownership of your home, you may decide to borrow against that equity for the purpose of home improvement, debt consolidation, or even to pay college tuition for your children. Lower credit scores will not only affect your ability to take out a home equity line of credit (HELOC), but you will also have to pay higher interest rates and other upfront costs if you are approved.

Credit Scores Affect Much More Than Mortgage Payments – 15 More Ways Consumers Suffer

What other ways can low credit scores affect consumers? While I am certain a comprehensive list could contain as many as a hundred items, here's a list of fifteen more ways in which consumers are suffering the cost of low credit scores.

1. **Lost Opportunity.** After hearing the stories of thousands of people, I know the biggest and most heartbreaking cost of poor credit is *Lost Opportunity*. It's not just that the rates and/or fees will be high. It's that certain people are simply unable to qualify for loan approval. Case closed and door slammed. This cost is truly immeasurable and involves those individuals being forced to live without, or never even having the opportunity for what they want. They may never get the job they want. Never reap the benefits of home ownership. Never experience the smell of a new car in their driveway. These are real issues that millions of Americans face each and every day.

2. **Humiliation.** If you've ever been turned down for credit, you've had a taste of what poor credit really feels like. It's pretty miserable to sweat every time you try to use a gas card; when your credit card is declined at a restaurant; when you have to "explain" every time you apply for a purchase, a subscription, or a service; or when you have a good job but you're excluded from being able to use a company credit card. Such humiliation causes despair and depression. There's no reason for anyone to go through this kind of hopelessness and humiliation; especially when there are simple steps you can take to avoid this kind of unnecessary frustration.

3. **Employment Opportunities.** Just as not having a specific degree can shut you out of certain jobs, so too can your credit. More and more, getting hired, promoted, or receiving a company credit card depends upon having strong credit scores and reports. In fact, a

large percentage of consumers who come to me for credit counseling are well-educated, upwardly mobile individuals who've been turned down for professional jobs because of their credit situation. Many have lost three months or more of their time interviewing for a job they ultimately did not get. Moreover, there is NO WAY that any person can be hired by a government facility, banking, lending, insurance, advising, or accounting firm if they have problematic credit scores or reports. It doesn't matter how much the employer likes you. Company policies and procedures are rapidly incorporating mandates of strong credit reports and scores.

4. **Medical Emergencies.** In the imminent future, hospitals will likely pull your credit scores to determine your ability to pay your medical bills. It is called MedFICO and I talk about it more in Chapter 5. Developers of this new system say the scores will not be used to decide whether or not treatment should be given. However, considering the flaws associated with the current scoring system, how can consumers be sure? Literally, this could be a matter of life or death. This concern is as true as it is serious, and it provides yet another reason why staying on top of your credit is so important.

5. **Auto Loans.** You've seen the ads, the ones that promise low, low, low interest rates with no money down for that brand new luxury car, and with a monthly payment of just $199! What a great deal, right? Then there's that really teeny, tiny writing at the bottom of the screen that says that the deal depends on good credit. If consumer credit scores are not impeccable, they will pay a very high interest rate. Up to 28% or more. They will also have to put a lot more money down.

   Unfortunately, low credit scores force individuals to pay in cold, hard cash, or suffer punitive interest rates. This is cash they could use for other necessities. Adding insult to injury, paying cash does nothing for consumer credit scores; however, a healthy installment loan is crucial to two major factors that make up consumer credit scores.

6. **Educational Loans.** Parents want to give their kids the best of everything, and most families rely on lines of credit or savings to fund their children's college education. But when you are forced to pay

more for *everything* because of poor credit scores, saving for college is virtually impossible. And once again, seeking a line of credit based on home equity isn't a viable option either. If you have low credit scores and pay a high interest rate on your existing mortgage, lenders will consider you a risk as you seek to incur more debt.

7. **Business Ownership.** Entrepreneurship–Being your own boss!–has long been one of the items high on the list of American Dreams. Yet because of lower credit scores, for many consumers, entrepreneurship will remain merely a dream.

You may have a stellar business plan and the commitment to put your stake in a profitable venture as an entrepreneur, but if your credit scores are low, lenders will approach you with caution, hindering the process, depleting the excitement. As always, the higher the score the better your chances are to secure an interest rate that won't cut into your potential profits.

8. **Surety Bonds**. When applying for a business license, most state governments require a surety bond to guarantee that the licensed individual will operate his or her business in accord with state regulations.

Because the surety bond industry assumes a 0% loss ratio, only those with good credit are approved (often times, credit scores above 660 are required.) And those who do not meet the credit score guidelines will pay 8-10% or more, which could make the difference in whether or not they can obtain or renew a business license.

9. **Checking Accounts.** Many banks will not open a checking account if you have poor credit scores; particularly if you have an NSF (non-sufficient fund) record filed against you that hasn't been handled. Day-to-day living can become very difficult and inconvenient if you have to pay cash for everything.

10. **Credit Cards.** We live in a world that's very difficult to navigate without credit cards. Let's face it, you can't rent a car without a credit card in hand, much less order airline tickets or other items over the phone or online. Low credit scores result in denial, or, if approved, suffer the highest interest rates. If you have low credit scores, you could be paying up to 30% financing on your credit

cards. Additionally, consumers with low credit scores tend to pay setup fees, account maintenance fees, and higher annual fees that are often waived for customers with good credit scores.

11. **Renting An Apartment Or Home.** Landlords like to get paid, and they won't rent to someone they think they will have to hunt down every month or worry that the rent check will bounce. And that's exactly why a landlord checks your credit standing before he or she signs an agreement with you. It doesn't matter if you have a strong payment history with former landlords, or a big paycheck. If your scores are low, you will have to pay a higher security deposit and will most likely require a co-signer.

12. **Renting A Car.** Car rental agencies are now pulling credit reports if someone wants to rent a car using a bank debit card rather than a credit card.

13. **Utilities.** More of the same. If you have low credit scores, your utility deposit will be higher than for those with good credit. As with renting an apartment, you may also be required to have a co-signer on the account.

14. **Insurance Rates And Options.** Many auto insurance companies now use credit scores to determine payments and payment schedules. Studies show that consumers with poor credit histories are more likely to file claims (which makes no logical sense at all.) Large insurance companies charge poor-credit consumers as much as three times the rate for consumers with excellent credit.

Having lower credit scores also reduces your option to negotiate a payment plan for your premium. If you are considered a high-risk client, the insurance company can demand that your annual premium be paid in full as a one-time payment. This is something most consumers can't afford.

15. **Less—Or No, Retirement Savings.** When you spend all of your money on high interest rates, or have to pay cash for everything, you have an incredible hurdle in saving for retirement. Your quality of life will suffer at a time when you would hope to relax and enjoy life.

THE REAL DEAL

The single first step you can take toward planning for a more secure future is to ensure you derive the very best value from every financial commitment you make. The best value means NOT spending hundreds or thousands of dollars on high interest rates for credit cards, auto loans, and mortgages.

Strong credit scores are the golden ticket to financial freedom for right NOW, and it prepares the foundation for financial security LATER. Isn't that what we all want? Planning for tomorrow by improving your situation today, you can eliminate the risk of limited financial security that comes from spending too much.

The good news is that loans can always be refinanced and credit card interest rates can be renegotiated. If you find yourself in a position of having to pay higher rates on credit cards, auto loans and mortgages due to low credit scores, once you get your credit back on track you will be in a good position to refinance and renegotiate with your creditors.

Remember, the key to good planning starts with good understanding. It starts with paying attention to what is happening with your credit report, and to what is happening in the financial world around you.

[1] http://www.nabe.com/publib/pol/08/03/pol0803.pdf
[2] https://www.efanniemae.com/sf/guides/ssg/annltrs/pdf/2008/0818.pdf

CHAPTER 5

Where Do Credit Reports And Scores Come From & How Many Do I Really Have?

Now that you know the costs and casualties of low credit scores and poor credit, let's talk about where credit scores come from, and cover some basic questions about credit reports and scores.

Although credit scoring has been around since the 1950s, it wasn't until the 1980s that it hit mainstream in the United States. Before that, lenders would use human judgment and personal opinion when evaluating a credit report to make a decision on an applicant's ability to repay debt. Not only was this a very slow process, it was unreliable because of human error. Fewer loans were made and it was much more difficult to qualify for financing than it is today.

The History Of The Credit Report

Where did those reports come from that lenders based their judgments on? It all started in 1898 with two brothers who owned a grocery store in Chattanooga, Tennessee. Cator and Guy Woolford assembled credit records of local residents and created what they called, The Merchant Guide, which they sold to retailers for $25 per year. Retailers used the information as an indicator of consumer creditworthiness. Sounds to me like the making of the first credit report!

The Merchant Guide was so successful that the Woolfords set out to make credit reporting their career. Eventually their company, originally called Retail Credit, became Equifax, one of the nation's three major credit reporting agencies.

As with any successful business idea, you can imagine that hundreds of entrepreneurs followed in the footsteps of Retail Credit hoping to profit on the great idea of selling credit reports to lenders and banking institutions. However, only three credit reporting agencies have truly prevailed: The Big Three. Equifax, Experian, and TransUnion (also known as "The Credit Bureaus.")

The Credit Bureaus — Who Exactly Are The Big Three?

Mistakenly referred to as the "Government," the "IRS," the "devil," and many other names that would not be appropriate to list in this book, I have found that one of the biggest consumer misconceptions in credit is who the three credit bureaus really are.

The word "bureau" in the Encyclopedia refers to "public office, government agency, news bureau." No wonder there's so much confusion.

The credit bureaus are NOT government agencies. They do not work for banks or creditors, and they are not paid to make your life miserable—it just feels that way. They are three companies that saw a vision of huge profits to be made by collecting data about YOU from your creditors and reselling that data to prospective lenders, employers, insurance companies, utility companies, and, most recently, to YOU, the consumer.

Today, all credit reports have one thing in common: The Big Three. All credit report vendors get their data from these three credit reporting agencies. So I think it's extremely important that you familiarize yourself with who they are, and where they came from. I think you will be quite amused. I know I was.

What Is Equifax?

As mentioned above, Equifax was originally founded as the Retail Credit Company in 1898 by Cator and Guy Woolford.

After their initial success selling credit information to local retailers, the company continued to expand with 300 branch offices and nearly 1,400 satellite offices. In the mid-1960s Retail Credit took the first steps toward automation. They took 3″ x 5″ index cards bearing information on thousands of consumers and converted it into an electronic database, which proved to be the company's greatest asset.

In 1979, they changed their name to Equifax, Inc. and strengthened their reporting operations by buying up smaller companies. Today the company, headquartered in Atlanta, Georgia, employs approximately 6,900 people in 14 countries throughout North America, Latin America and Europe. They currently maintain data on more than 300 million consumers and 100 million businesses worldwide.

What Is Experian?

If you come from my generation or before, then you probably recognize the name TRW. In order to understand the relationship of TRW and Experian, I'll have to go back a little in history.

Thompson **R**amo **W**ooldridge Inc. (TRW), was founded in 1901 as the Cleveland Cap Screw Co. It began by making cap screws, bolts, and studs, but soon its main product was welded valves for cars made by automotive pioneer Alexander Winton.

In the mid-1960s, TRW launched its Information Services division and started compiling a consumer database. Like Equifax, the company grew by purchasing smaller businesses and continued to expand. By the mid-1980s, the company had a firm position as the largest credit reporting agency in the United States with credit histories on file of approximately 90 million Americans.

However, in the early 1990s, an article in *The Wall Street Journal* accused TRW of sloppy procedures and inadequate response to consumer complaints. These accusations resulted in a multitude of lawsuits, most of which were remedied; however, at that point TRW decided to sell off the Information Services division, and the first buyer in line was a company called Experian, founded in 1980 by a man named John Pace in Nottingham, England.

Prior to 1996, when Experian acquired its U.S. credit reporting business from TRW, Experian's business was in marketing solutions, decision analytics and interactive services, collecting information on people, businesses, motor vehicles, insurance, and lifestyle data.

The company, currently employing more than 4,500 people in North America, maintains credit information on approximately 215 million consumers and more than 15 million businesses in the United States. The firm provides address information for more than 20 billion promotional mail pieces sent out to more than 100 million households annually.

What Is TransUnion?

TransUnion was formed in 1968 to be the parent holding company for the Union Tank Car Company, a railcar leasing operation.

They entered into the credit reporting business in 1969, when they acquired the Credit Bureau of Cook County (CBCC), which manually maintained 3.6 million card files in 400 seven-drawer cabinets.

In the early 1970s, TransUnion– creating the tape-to-disc transfer which drastically cut the time and cost to update consumer files–became the first company in the credit reporting industry to revolutionize the transfer of consumer data between the creditors and the credit bureaus.

Throughout the 1970s and 1980s, they continued to expand their facilities and capabilities through investments in technology and strategic growth initiatives and acquisitions. In 1988 they achieved full coverage in the United States, maintaining and updating information on virtually every market-active consumer in the country.

Today, TransUnion reaches businesses and consumers in 25 countries on 5 continents, and they maintain credit histories on an estimated 500 million consumers around the globe.

The History Of The Credit Score — Who Is Fair Isaac & Co. (FICO)?

In 1956, an engineer named Bill Fair and a mathematician named Earl Isaac saw a great opportunity to fill the need in the credit reporting industry for an objective scoring system that would analyze all of the data about consumers quickly and with greater accuracy than human judgment and personal opinion. So with an investment of $400 each, they started on a plan to create the first credit scoring system. Their company was called Fair Isaac & Co. (FICO).

Between 1956 and 1980, Fair Isaac & Co. implemented its scoring software into the European Banking System. After much success in Europe, the credit scoring system hit mainstream in the United States in 1989, debuting at Equifax.

In 1991, TransUnion and Experian came on board. These three major credit reporting agencies, Experian, Equifax, and TransUnion worked with Fair Isaac & Co. to implement an objective scoring system that would analyze all available data on any given individual, and then compare it against the national average of consumer spending habits. A 3-digit scoring system was developed to rate individuals with scores between 300 and 850 that would quantify his or her ability to pay back money borrowed on a loan.

> ### FACT
>
> It's important to understand that Fair Isaac & Co. itself does not store data on consumers and they cannot change your credit scores or keep a record of them. They simply provide the analytical tools and solutions to determine credit scores.

Today, credit scores generated using the Fair Isaac & Co. FICO scoring software are the most used credit bureau scores in the world, with more than 100 billion scores sold to date.

How Many Scores Do You Have & Which Ones Count?

You have one score.

You have one plus score.

You have one true FICO score.

All scores are FICO scores.

Only the scores from the three credit bureaus matter.

Etc. Etc. Etc.

Do any of these sound familiar?

Many consumers believe that there is only one credit score. This is not true. Every individual has three credit scores that are used by both lending and non-lending industries. These scores are generated from the data stored at the three credit bureaus: Equifax, Experian, and TransUnion.

Where it gets confusing is that there are hundreds of versions of these three credit scores generated from this data and sold to consumers and lenders by hundreds of different credit score vendors. As I will discuss in more detail below, every credit score vendor uses the same data from each credit bureau, however, they all use different software to calculate those scores.

When it comes to applying for a loan, consumers have no idea of which scores will be used. This makes it crucial for consumers to consistently check and manage the data that is being reported about them to each individual credit bureau.

The Credit Distribution Tree

Understanding the different aspects of the credit scoring process can be difficult to get your head around. The following charts use a graphic presentation to illustrate how credit gets distributed. These credit distribution trees should help you understand how there can be so many versions of your three credit scores and reports.

The Data

The process starts with a transfer of data from the creditors to the credit bureaus regarding your payment history. This transfer of information is implemented through a tape-to-disc transfer and occurs as follows:

- On open installment and revolving accounts, every 30, 60 or 90 days, depending on the individual creditor's reporting procedures.

- On negative payment history as it relates to collections, charge-offs, and public records, usually within 60-90 days of occurrence.

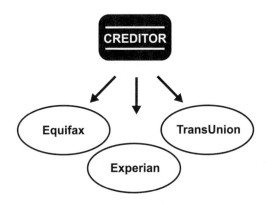

The Credit Bureaus

- They store your data individually, and do not share that data.

- They update your file whenever the creditor reports. Many creditors do not report to all three credit bureaus, so the information being stored will vary.

- They do not store your credit score. The information in your credit report changes often. Your scores are calculated each time your credit report is pulled.

- They sell your data to Businesses and Consumers in the following ways:

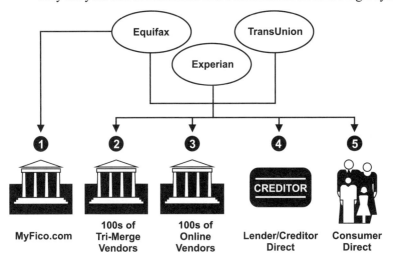

Summary:

1. Equifax sends data to MyFico.com, which I will talk about later in this Chapter.

2. All three credit bureaus sell data to 100s of Tri-Merge Vendors. Tri-Merge Vendors are companies who sell credit reports and credit scores to Businesses (i.e. mortgage companies, auto lenders, insurance companies, banks.) Tri-Merge Vendors would include Landsafe, Kroll Data, and Info 1 as examples.

3. All three credit bureaus also sell data to 100s of Online Vendors.

Online Vendors are companies who sell credit reports and credit scores to consumers directly.

4. All three credit bureaus also sell credit reports and credit scores to businesses direct who use those reports to make lending decisions (i.e. mortgage lenders, auto lenders and banks.)

5. Finally, all three credit bureaus sell credit reports and/or scores to consumers directly.

FACT

The three credit bureaus are the only companies who store your data. In all instances above, the data is fed real-time at the time your credit report is pulled.

Third-Party Vendors

MyFico.com, Tri-Merge Vendors, and Online Vendors are considered Third-Party Vendors because once they receive your credit information from the three credit bureaus they then sell your credit reports and scores as follows:

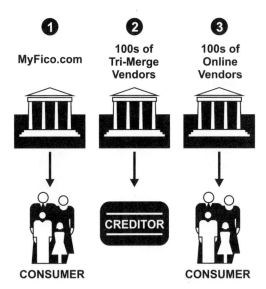

Summary:

1. MyFico.com sells credit reports and scores to millions of consumers directly.

2. Tri-Merge Vendors sell credit reports and scores to hundreds of thousands of businesses directly that use those credit reports and scores to making lending and non-lending financial decisions about millions of consumers.

3. Online Vendors sell credit reports and scores to millions of consumers directly.

What's The Difference?

As the charts show, there are four channels by which businesses and consumers can access credit scores. They are:

*   MyFico.com (AKA: True Fico Score)

*   The Credit Bureau Score (AKA: Equifax, Experian and Trans-Union)

*   Online Score

*   Tri-Merge Score (AKA: Lender Score)

Let's talk about the differences.

The True Fico Score

Credit scores are almost always referred to as FICO scores. This creates some confusion because most people do NOT actually get a true FICO score; rather, they get a score generated from a modified version of the true FICO model.

There are only two places to get true FICO scores: from MyFico.com, the consumer division of Fair Isaac & Co., the creator of the credit scoring software; and from Equifax. Even though all three credit bureaus license the software from Fair Isaac & Co., only Equifax has stayed 100% true to the FICO model.

Why would you want a true FICO score? As many as 90% of U.S. lenders use the FICO model to make lending decisions. Thus this score is the most realistic one that can be purchased directly.

If that's the case, why wouldn't you *always* purchase a true FICO score? Credit reports and scores purchased from MyFico.com are more expensive than most online consumer credit report vendors.

When is it a good idea to purchase a true FICO score? Before applying for a loan. This is the best way to know what lenders will base their terms on. FICO scores are generally the best indicator of credit worthiness and a good overall indicator of where your credit (mortgage, credit card, auto, etc.) stands.

Does it hurt your credit scores to pull a true FICO score? No.

The Credit Bureau Score

You already know that the credit bureaus use software created by Fair Isaac & Co. to calculate credit scores. Although Equifax uses the exact FICO model, the other two credit bureaus have made minor modifications to the software to be unique and to do what they believe gives them a competitive edge. They do so by selling different formatted credit reports, and by calling their credit reports and credit scores different names.

- Experian sells the "PLUS Score."
- TransUnion sells the "TrueCredit" score.
- Equifax sells the "Score Power" score.

What is the benefit of purchasing a credit bureau score? It's a preference. Some people feel more comfortable going directly to the source of the data.

Why wouldn't you always purchase a credit bureau score? Because to get the full picture, you would have to purchase a credit report and score from each credit bureau individually (three transactions vs. one). Each credit bureau will offer to sell you all three credit scores to try to keep all of your business; however, if you order all three credit scores from one credit bureau, you must realize that those scores are being calculated using that credit bureau's version of the FICO model. So the Equifax score that you receive from Experian will not be the real Equifax score.

When would you want to purchase a credit bureau score? If you are not comfortable purchasing from an unknown online company. Again, it's a matter of preference.

Does it hurt your credit scores to pull a credit bureau score? No.

The Online Score

There are hundreds if not thousands of online companies that offer credit reports to consumers. They offer multiple ways to get your reports. You can get all three reports and one credit score, all three reports and three credit scores, or one report and one credit score. In all cases, the data is taken from all three credit bureaus, and the scores are calculated by applying very general criteria that is not specific to any one use. As a result, the scores generated by these online companies are usually unrealistic when it comes to lending and are therefore not a good source for you to make a determination about how a particular type of lender would view you. Hopefully this will change.

Why would you want online scores? For credit maintenance and credit watch purposes, they are more affordable.

Why wouldn't you always purchase online scores? Because the scores generated by these companies are not realistic to the lending industry. Also, the information offered on these reports is incomplete. You don't get the full picture.

When would you want to purchase online scores? If a consumer signs up for an annual program that generates an updated report every 30 days, it provides an opportunity to monitor credit scores at a reasonable cost. Annual programs also monitor credit reports for identity theft.

Does it hurt your credit scores to pull an online report? No.

The Lender Score (aka: Tri-Merge)

When you apply for a home or auto loan or any type of revolving credit, the scores pulled by lenders are not the same scores that you receive from the credit bureaus directly or from online companies.

Most lenders purchase their credit reports and scores from a third-party vendor. There are literally hundreds of companies that offer this service to mortgage companies, auto lenders, and banks. Some commonly known companies that generate tri-merge reports are Landsafe, Info1, and Kroll Factual Data, to name a few. This is how it works:

Let's say a consumer goes to ABC Mortgage Company to apply for a home loan. ABC Mortgage Company asks the potential borrower to fill out an application that authorizes them to pull credit reports and credit scores. ABC Mortgage Company uses Landsafe as its credit report vendor. The loan originator at ABC Mortgage goes online and accesses the ABC Mortgage account with Landsafe. The borrower's credit application is then entered into the system. From there, Landsafe's automated system contacts the three credit bureaus who, in turn, respond with a data feed. Once the data on the borrower is fed back into Landsafe's system, Landsafe generates a credit score for each credit bureau.

So, as you can see, all lenders calculate credit scores using the *same data* from the three credit bureaus, but all lenders DO NOT use the *same software* to evaluate that data.

Lenders calculate scores based on criteria considered to be the most pertinent for evaluating creditworthiness as it relates to their unique programs.

Lender scores are not sold to consumers directly. Sometimes your lender can give you a copy of the report that the lending company pulled, but it all depends on the company's agreement with the tri-merge company the lender works with. It doesn't hurt to ask. Just remember that reading a tri-merge report is much different than reading an individual report.

Does it hurt your credit scores when a lender pulls it? Yes. We will talk about how much it hurts your scores in Chapter 11.

What Is A MedFICO Score?

A company named Healthcare Analytics is designing a credit scoring system for hospitals to determine whether patients are capable of paying medical bills. Development of this program is supported jointly by Fair Isaac & Co. and Tenet Healthcare Corp., a leader in the healthcare industry.

The idea behind MedFICO is to pull the credit reports after treatment, not before, so that hospitals can determine whether or not they should write off unpaid bills as uncollectible, bad debt. Why? Because hospitals are better able to balance expenses against revenue and invest in new ventures if they can more accurately gauge whether or not bills will be paid. The problem is that there is no guarantee. With legislation so far behind, it could be years before a new model contains regulations that force compliance with the FCRA.

Should you be worried? As an expert, I say yes, and here's why: Rumors are swirling that amendments to the Fair Credit Reporting Act are currently under consideration. As we know, the existing legislation currently has many flaws, so how do they expect to regulate and monitor newcomers to the system? And we're not talking about a voluntary credit check (as would be the case for a new car or for a house). We're talking about an emergency, one that catches you completely by surprise—a life-threatening emergency. This development is extremely disconcerting and it elevates the importance of credit monitoring to a critical level.

What Is An Insurance Score?

Some auto insurance companies rely on an Insurance Score. The Insurance Score is very similar to the traditional FICO score. The good news: If you have a high FICO score, you will also have a high insurance score.

What Is Vantage Score?

This is a newly developed program that is backed by the three credit bureaus: Equifax, Experian, and TransUnion. They jointly created Vantage Score in order to have their own scoring software program so they wouldn't have to subscribe to Fair Isaac & Co. (FICO), which owns the scoring software that all credit report vendors use.

To avoid copyright infringement, and to differentiate Vantage from FICO's existing scoring system (which has fallen under a lot of criticism in the media), the three credit bureaus sought to create a completely different product. Vantage uses a numeric scale of 501-990, and also a parallel alphabetic scale that classifies consumers into fixed A, B, C, D, and F grades.

But the Vantage system does not appear to be catching on as a mainstream product. The United States and several other countries have spent billions of dollars implementing the FICO system into business and commerce. It would be an enormous undertaking and an extraordinary expense to change the way lenders score us. Every lender, creditor and mortgage company would have to implement brand new systems and procedures. In my opinion, it's not going to happen any time in the near future. It's just too big of an undertaking.

And by the way, consumers are just now starting to understand the FICO system. Can you imagine having to start all over again?

What Is Beacon And NextGen?

Beacon and NextGen are not scores. They are versions of the FICO software. Just like when you purchase an update for your computer software.

Beacon (aka: Classic FICO) is the original version of the FICO software, and NextGen 2.0 is the most recent version of the FICO software. The significant differences in my opinion are as follows:

- For the lender, the new model (NextGen 2.0) has 80 predictive variables, more than twice the number in the original Beacon model. This may be good for lenders, however, again—for consumers—doubling the variables only makes the reality of consumers meeting the high standards of the credit scoring system even more difficult.

- For consumers, the most significant change is the increase in the de-duplication period for auto and mortgage inquiries from 14 days to 45 days. De-duplication is the window of time in which consumers can have their credit pulled by as many auto and mortgage lenders as they want and it will only be counted as one hard inquiry. An important point to remember here is that not all credit report vendors have updated their software to the NextGen 2.0 model. I always advise my clients to ask the lender which version of the software they are using to pull their credit. This way they will know whether or not they are going to be hit with a hard inquiry. I talk about this in more detail in Chapter 11.

THE REAL DEAL

The credit scoring system has a generations-long history. From very humble, pre-technology beginnings early developers sought to help quantify the risk of loaning an individual money. Today, these systems are still widely used on a grand and global scale. This stringing along of seemingly arcane practices makes much of the credit scoring system seem unnecessarily complicated, and not the least bit intuitive.

Thus you need to understand the background that put the systems into place. It is important for you to understand how it all comes together, and how all of these big businesses compile the decision-making information that has master power over your financial future.

Understanding how the credit scoring industry compiles your information will give you a better understanding of how information gets processed, as well as how mistakes happen. The ultimate goal is that this important information will help you be a wiser, better-educated consumer who will know where to go for information and help when there's a problem.

CHAPTER 6

Credit Score Basics

Credit reporting and scoring is not the least bit intuitive, and that's just the way the reporting bureaus like it. Confusion creates dependence, not to mention fear. This important chapter provides concrete answers to the most frequently asked questions about credit scores.

What Is The Range For Credit Scores?

Credit scores range from 300–850. The higher the score, the better deal you will get. Keep in mind that while many lenders use credit scores to help them make lending decisions, every lender has its own strategy, including the level of risk it finds acceptable for a given credit product. There is no single "cutoff score" used by all lenders.

What Is A Good Credit Score?

The bar for "good" credit continues to be raised. Less than a year ago, a credit score of 680 was considered to be "great." However, the credit crisis that came out of the subprime mortgage issue has lenders tightening their standards. As of this writing, "excellent" credit now comes with a credit score of 740 or better. But here is the range of rating scores as it applies to consumer average:

>
> 300 to 559   BAD
>
> 560 to 659   NOT GOOD
>
> 660 to 724   GOOD
>
> 725 to 759   VERY GOOD
>
> 760 to 850   GREAT

Under current economic conditions, scores higher than 740 are ideal.

This new standard is troubling. It raises the bar very high for people to achieve good credit. As a credit expert, I have seen very few credit scores over 740. I know how extremely difficult it will be for people to maintain this higher standard. However, I do believe that, over time, standards will lighten up. But, until then, consumers need to learn everything they can about achieving good credit, and must take the steps to get there.

Why Do Credit Scores From The Three Credit Bureaus Vary?

Credit scores between the credit bureaus can vary by as much as 100 points or more. This is because not all creditors report all of your credit to all three credit bureaus, and since the credit bureaus are competitors they DO NOT share data with one another. This explains why the scores vary as each line item affects the score either up or down. It's important to make sure that all credit bureaus are reporting your *"good credit."*

Why Don't I Have A Credit Score(s)?

Some of the reasons that would cause a consumer not to generate a credit score or credit report are as follows:

• They don't have a social security number.

• They are not over the age of 18.

• They don't have enough credit. It takes at least one credit account that has been open 4-6 months to produce credit scores.

• Their open accounts have not been active for 6 months.

• Their credit reports are only showing negative credit. No open positive accounts.

• They are being reported as deceased.

• The information entered to pull their report is incomplete.

• They have a fraud alert on their credit file.

> **CREDIT TIP**
>
> If you know that you have open active credit but are not gener-
> ating a credit report or credit score, it usually means there is an
> identification problem with the credit bureau. Call the credit bu-
> reau directly and, after a couple of identification questions, they
> will tell you what the problem is so that you can rectify it.

Do Lenders Use All Three Scores?

Mortgage lenders use the middle of the three credit scores. In most cases,
when it comes to a joint account application for mortgage, the lender will
use the lower of the two middle scores.

> **WORD OF CAUTION**
>
> Most consumers believe that mortgage lenders and other credi-
> tors use the average of the three credit scores. This is NEVER
> the case when it comes to lending decisions.

All other creditors can use any one of the three, but more and more creditors are starting to pull all three.

How Fast Can Your Credit Scores Change?

Your credit scores are a snapshot of the moment. They can change whenever
the information on your credit report changes. The good news is that once
it changes, yesterday's score is non-existent and you don't have to worry
about your past haunting you.

What Goes Into Your Credit Scores?

Many consumers think that as long as they pay their bills on time they will
automatically have high credit scores. That's not how it works. Obviously,
paying your bills on time is important; but understanding the factors that make
up your credit scores is your key to maintaining good credit, as well as your
key to taking immediate and lifelong steps toward credit improvement.

If you manage each factor properly, the basic formula is easy to understand and is a powerful tool.

FACT

The exact formula for calculating your credit scores **is not public**, and probably never will be. It is under U.S. Patent Law, and only Fair Isaac & Co. has access to the formula.

According to Fair Isaac & Co., the creator of the scoring system, there are five factors that go into calculating credit scores. The following pie chart is a guideline as to how much each factor is considered:

What Makes Up Your Credit Score?

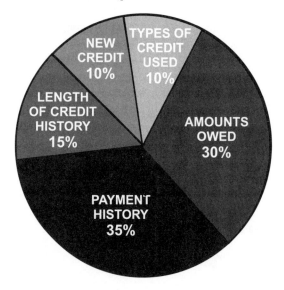

What Is Not Considered In Your Credit Scores?

• Your race, color, religion, national origin

• Sex and marital status

- Age

- Salary, occupation, title, employer, date employed, employment history

- Where you live

- Interest rates

- Dollar amounts

- Any items reported as child/family support obligations or rental agreements (unless they become delinquent)

- Soft inquiries

- Information not proven to be predictive of future credit performance

- Whether or not you are participating in a credit counseling program of any kind

THE REAL DEAL

The myriad details of the credit scoring system can make you feel like you're knee deep in alphabet soup. But trust me, it is a very worthwhile endeavor that will reward you with a brighter financial future.

When you take the time to understand the who's and what's of good credit, you will be well prepared to improve and maintain your highest possible credit scores. Now that you have a background on the makeup of the credit scoring system, it's time to dig deep into the factors that make up your score.

The following chapters contain an abundance of important information that can help you gain an in-depth understanding of the cast of characters that make up the credit scoring universe. The information will provide you with an extensive education regarding each and every facet of the five factors of credit and how you can improve each to achieve your maximum credit scores.

CHAPTER 7

The Five Factors Of Credit: Part One - Amounts Owed

30% is Amounts Owed (aka: Using Revolving & Installment Debt) - Worth 255 Points

It has been widely reported that household debt is skyrocketing as incomes are actually shrinking. The Federal Reserve, The Consumer Federation of America, and many other sites that consumers refer to for information on this topic are quoting statistics that will make your jaw drop. Throw into that mix that personal bankruptcies have become next to impossible and the monthly minimum payment on credit cards have doubled, and you have a perfect storm for consumer debt to consume individuals and families.

Those numbers may be alarming, but they don't matter when it comes to your credit scores. I agree that it is time to take this bull by the horns and get a handle on consumer debt, but that's going to take awhile. What matters today is learning how to manage credit wisely and to start paying your debt in a way that will allow you to maximize your credit scores and help you avoid making innocent mistakes that can drop your scores by 100 points instantly.

There is a strategy to everything, and when it comes to paying credit card debts, the strategies in this section will help you achieve an increase in your credit scores when you need it the most.

What This Factor Considers

This factor, Amounts Owed, is a record of all of your debt and how you manage that debt. This factor is broken down into two categories:

1. **Revolving Debt** – credit cards, revolving loan accounts, and some home equity lines of credit

2. **Installment Debt** – mortgage loans, auto loans, student loans, and home equity lines of credit

Scores are impacted when a high percentage of your available credit is being used. This gives the impression that you are overextended, making you at risk for paying late or not at all.

In my experience of working with thousands of credit score improvement cases, I am going to say that 25% of this factor is allocated toward **Revolving Debt**, and only 5% is allocated toward **Installment Debt**.

Per Fair Isaac & Co., when calculating your score, this factor considers the following elements:

• Amount owing on accounts

• Amount owing on specific types of accounts

• Lack of a specific type of balance

• Number of accounts with balances

• Proportion of credit lines used (proportion of balances to total credit limits on certain types of revolving accounts)

• Proportion of installment loan amounts still owing (proportion of balance to original loan amount on certain types of installment loans)

Tips For Improving The Amounts Owed Factor

Fortunately, the Amounts Owed Factor is one the easiest factors to correct and control. By implementing the following tips, you will maximize your potential for higher credit scores in this area:

1. In order to prove to the scoring system that you know how to manage revolving debt, *you MUST have active credit card accounts*.

   I agree with most financial experts who say that not using credit cards is better for your budget. Especially for those who do not have discipline when it comes to spending. And my opinion of the credit card industry today is that it is out of control and underregulated and until serious changes are made to legislation, I would prefer to advise my clients NOT to use credit cards, however, Fair Isaac & Co., the creator of our credit scoring system says that without revolving accounts, consumers cannot maximize their credit scores. *There is no getting around it.*

So the advice I give to my clients is to look at their credit cards *as tools*, not luxuries. Unless they must have access to a credit card for business, they should use the card for gas and groceries – THAT'S ALL. In addition, as you will read later in this chapter, the dollar amount of the limit does not influence the credit score one way or the other—it is the balance-to-limit ratio that matters. Point: When adding a new credit card account, apply for a low limit—one that doesn't leave room for overspending.

If you do not have a credit card, here are some tips on how to get one:

- **Go To Your Bank or Credit Union First.** I always have my clients go to their bank first. Whether you have an es-tablished relationship with a representative or not, it is wise to go into the bank directly. Do not try to inquire or apply over the telephone. In most instances, bank and lender cus-tomer service representatives are located in different states and sometimes different countries. It's very likely they don't have a clue about the products offered by individual branches.

  Ask what type of accounts they offer for clients who are trying to build or re-establish credit. Be direct. Tell them what your credit scores are so they can tell you if you qualify before they pull your report. You do not want to incur a hard inquiry (see Chapter 11) if you can avoid it.

  If your bank does offer a credit card program, make sure they report to all three credit bureaus every 30 days. This is very important. You'll find that most major banks and credit unions do.

- **A Secured Credit Card Is A Great Option!** If your bank does not have such a program, or does not report to all three credit bureaus every 30 days, then it is time for you to apply for secured credit card. For new credit users, or consumers who have filed for bankruptcy, or have closed all of their credit card accounts, a secured credit card is a very good option.

A secured credit card means that you put up your own money as collateral. It looks and works just like a regular credit card, and is considered a major credit card by the scoring system.

CREDIT TIP

The amount of the limit does not matter to the scoring system. A $500 limit is rated the same as a $5,000 limit. It's the ratio between the balance and limit that is considered, which I talk about next. Point: It is not necessary to deposit more than the minimum amount required—usually $300.

I have seen credit scores increase by as much as 50-60 points in the first two months of my clients using a secured account. And after managing your credit card account and paying it on time, you can ask for your initial deposit back, at which time that account becomes a regular unsecured account.

WORD OF CAUTION

Stay away from department store cards and pre-approved offers that you receive in the mail. When trying to rebuild or establish credit, you should apply for a major credit card ONLY. I will talk about this more in Chapter 10.

- **Become An Authorized User On A Family Member's or Spouse's Account.** With the new guidelines from FICO as outlined in the new Fair and Accurate Credit Transaction Act, there is a lot of controversy about whether or not authorized user accounts still help establish credit, and my experience proves that they do if you carry the same last name as the credit card owner.

As a true consumer advocate, my advice is to build your own credit if possible because that gives you power and control, but as a last resort this option will help. To maximize the benefit of this option, make sure that the account you are being added to belongs to someone you trust, has NO negative history reporting at all, has and keeps a balance under 30% of the limit and is at least 2-3 years old.

WORD OF CAUTION

Piggy-backing on a stranger's credit history is a mistake and it's fraud. It doesn't work anymore, and it will put you at risk.

2. The next step toward improving your score in this factor is to make sure that the following information is being reported accurately for each account:

    - Make sure that all of your open accounts and recently closed accounts with positive history are reported to all three credit bureaus. I emphasize positive, because if you have just had a recent late added to an account, or you are over the limit on a credit card, and you are about to enter into a loan transaction, you do not want to go out of your way to make the credit bureau aware of that negative account if it is not reporting.

    - Make sure that your credit limits are reporting to all three credit bureaus on all open credit card accounts, and closed accounts that still have balances. However, if accounts are closed and paid off, there is no need to worry about limits reporting.

WORD OF CAUTION

If you have a closed credit account that still has a balance, it is a negative to your credit scores. You should never close a credit card account with a balance, but if you have already closed it, or it has been closed by the creditor, then you should pay the balance off as soon as possible. If you cannot pay the balance off all at once, then these accounts should be managed in the same manner as your open accounts until paid in full.

- Make sure that the balances on your installment accounts are correct. Auto and mortgage lenders are notorious for being months behind on reporting updated balances to credit bureaus.

- Make sure that open dates on all accounts are accurate. As you will see in Chapter 9, Length of History makes up 15% of your credit scores.

3. **How you manage your credit card balances is one of the biggest secrets in this industry to improving your scores.** There are specific rules that the scoring system uses to rate revolving balances and they are:

- If you want your credit scores to improve, keep the balances on all credit cards under 30% of your available limits on statement date—consistently.

- If you want to maintain your credit scores, it's okay to keep the balances on all cards between 30-49% of your available limits on statement date.

WORD OF CAUTION

Once your balance goes over 50% of your available limit, you start losing points. According to Fair Isaac & Co., a maxed out credit card can cost up to 80 points, even if there is a good history on that account. Logic: Statistics show that individuals who carry a balance of over 50% on revolving accounts month to month, appear to be living off of their credit cards and are more likely to default on their payments. While this rationale does not make sense on low limit credit cards, all accounts are treated the same.

Statement date means the date your actual statement is printed or emailed to you. Not the due date. What most consumers don't realize is that the balance that is printed on your statement is the balance that gets reported to the credit bureaus and it is that balance to limit ratio that gets calculated in your score. So make sure that you find out from each of your revolving account creditors what date they print your statement, and make your payment before that date.

4. **If you have to charge more than the 30% or 50%** of your available limit as defined above, then make sure that you go home and pay that balance down immediately. Don't take any chances.

5. **If you cannot pay down your credit card balances to 30% or 50%** of your available limit as defined above 4-6 months prior to applying for a loan, call your credit card companies to ask for a temporary limit increase without pulling your credit. Tell them you are in the process of purchasing a home and that your balances are affecting your score. Some creditors will oblige if you have maintained a good payment history on the account.

6. **Pay credit card balances across the board**. In other words, it will not help your credit scores if you pay down one card at a time. So if you have three cards at 80% of their limit, and you cannot pay them down to 30% or 50% of your available limit as defined above all at once, pay them down in equal increments so the balances all decrease at the same rate.

7. **DO NOT consolidate your credit card debt** onto one low-interest

card UNLESS the balance on the new credit card (after the debt transfer) is under 30% or 50% of your available limit as defined above. Remember to continue to use your major credit cards for small purchases. Most accounts, if not used, will become unrated after 6 months.

8. **Don't close credit cards accounts at all**, if possible. If you feel you have too many accounts, then simply stop using all of the accounts. Let some of them become unrated. You will lose points in two factors when you close a credit card account, both in the Amounts Owed Factor (30%) where you will lose available limit, and in the Length of Credit History Factor (15%). These two factors combine to make up nearly half of your credit scores, so pay attention. A common misconception by consumers is that when you close a credit card account, any bad history on that account goes away. This is not the case. That history stays with you.

    The only time closing a credit card account should be considered is in the instance of divorce, identity theft, or removing your name from an authorized user account that has incurred negative history or has high balance-to-limit ratios.

9. **Don't open accounts you don't need**. Just because credit is offered to you, does not mean that you should accept it. When you receive one of those pre-approved credit card letters in the mail, in most instances your credit report has not yet been pulled, so you are NOT approved for the account. Once you pick up the phone to call the creditor, they will pull your report and you will be penalized immediately for the hard inquiry (10% of your score.) Then, the terms of the original offer they made will change based on your scores, and that 0% APR offer will turn into a 28% APR with additional fees and costs.

    It is best to avoid these types of special offer credit cards (including department store offers of "open an account today to save 15% off of your purchase.") The scoring system frowns upon third-party finance cards.

CREDIT TIP

I recommend that my clients Opt Out completely from receiving all marketing offers for new credit. This way, they avoid receiving unauthorized hard inquiries and remove the temptation to apply for credit they don't need. You can opt out by calling 1(888)5-OPTOUT, 1(888)567-8688.

10. **Installment loans are there for a reason,** so paying off your car loan early may be good for your budget but it will not improve your scores. In fact, it can actually pull down your scores because you will have one less active installment account in your credit mix. The scoring system wants to see that you can follow a payment agreement over a certain period of time (i.e. $250.00 per month for a period of 5 years with no late pays.)

11. **Don't go over your credit card limits,** even if by just one dollar. Doing so could cause you to lose 100 or more points, the result of a double penalty. The system interprets that you cannot hold to a creditor's agreement, and also that you are overextended. Both carry very negative impacts to your scores.

WORD OF CAUTION

Calling your credit company from the store to get approval will do you no good for approving an over-the-limit purchase. Sure, you might walk out with the merchandise, but the cost of the drop in your score will outweigh any pleasure you enjoyed from the purchase.

12. **Be careful with American Express cards** because most AMEX cards do not have a credit limit. As a result, the scoring system will use last month's statement total as your available credit limit. This means that if you spent $5,000 last month, and then $6,500 this month, it appears to the system that you are over your limit. The best way to handle AMEX is to make sure that you pay your bill before the statement date, without exception.

Real Life Success Story: John

John came to me with a 620 credit score. Other than a few aged late pays, he had a fairly decent credit history. For this reason, he could not understand why his credit scores were so low. After evaluating his reports, I quickly found a home equity line of credit, commonly called a HELOC account, mistakenly identified as a revolving account. This account had a limit of $49,000, and a balance due of $49,000. As a result, John appeared to have a credit card account that was maxed out.

Since a HELOC is actually a secured loan, I worked with the credit bureaus and the lender to change the type of account from "revolving" to "mortgage." The second preference for changing the type of account in this situation is "installment," but when that request is rejected, "other" is a good third choice. When I negotiated that single change, his scores shot up 75 points. Why? Because I removed the "over the limit revolving account" status from his profile.

John was able to see the big pop in his credit scores because he had strong credit in other areas.

THE REAL DEAL

How you manage your amounts owed has a tremendous impact on your credit scores. Remember, this factor accounts for a whopping 30% of your credit scores. In simple terms, this one factor has the potential to put you over the top when it comes to achieving credit scores high enough to get you preferential credit treatment. That's a tremendous incentive to understanding the specifics of the amounts owed factor. If you don't know the simple rules to play by, this one factor also has the potential to create a financial nightmare.

So check those reports, and make sure you keep your amounts owed well within the parameters set forth in this chapter. When you do, you can rest assured that 30% of your credit score is in good shape.

CHAPTER 8

The Five Factors Of Credit: Part Two - Payment History

35% Is Payment History - Worth 297.5 Points

How many times have you misplaced a bill, only to find it the day after the due date? You feel an instant knot in your stomach because you know you just incurred a big late charge penalty, you lost that favorable interest rate, and you will be dealt a nasty blow to your credit scores. *Payment history makes up 35% of your scores, the largest percentage in your credit reports.* You owe it to yourself to make sure that you understand everything you need to know about this factor and how you can keep this factor as high as possible.

Your payment history is your financial footprint, tracks of which indicate to potential creditors your history of how and when you pay your bills. It is the best indicator of your credit worthiness.

Late payments or missed payments are big red flags, each of which can wipe out as much as 80-100 points off your score. Creditors won't ask why you were late with your payments; they will simply deny you credit. It could be because you have lost your job, had a medical crisis, were on vacation, but it simply doesn't matter. They are going to assume that you are a high-risk borrower.

Lots of money in the bank and plenty of unused credit can't erase the dings from poor payment history. In fact, a big part of my business is a very wealthy crowd whose busy lifestyles and hands-off attitudes about paying their bills have caused their credit scores to go into the tank, despite their cash-rich bank accounts. Payment history indicates the level of care and responsibility you exercise to maintain your existing accounts.

What This Factor Considers

Payment history is more than just a record of payments made on your accounts. It also involves other important issues, ones that most likely you've not even considered. Nonetheless, they weigh heavily on your score.

Per Fair Isaac & Co., when calculating your score, this factor considers the following elements:

1. **Payment Information On Accounts** – This includes payment information on any credit cards you have, retail accounts (such as a department store credit cards), installment loans (auto loans or any loan that requires monthly payments), finance company credit accounts and mortgages. It includes the payments made and the dates they were made.

2. **Adverse Public Records** – This category reports any information on bankruptcies, wage garnishments, judgments, lawsuits and liens. If you have any public records on your credit report, these will cause your scores to drop instantly and significantly. But as with any negative account, the older the item, the less it will damage your credit scores. However, this category is the hardest to improve upon because it deals with the most severe credit problems; and some items in this category can stay on your report longer than the standard 7-Year Reporting Period, which I will talk about in Chapter 14.

3. **Severity Of Delinquency** – This category judges how severe the delinquency is, such as how late a payment was. Obviously, the sooner a late payment is made up, the better. A 30-day late payment will not count as much against you as a 60 or 90-day late payment, but even one 30-day late payment can ding your report up to 80 points.

4. **Amount Past Due On Any Account** – This is tied to the severity of delinquency category. If you have ANY AMOUNT showing in the Past Due column on open and closed accounts, it can cost you dearly.

5. **Recentness Of Past Due Items And Delinquencies, Adverse Records, Or Collection Items** – This category takes into consideration how recent the derogatory is on each account.

CREDIT TIP

The older a derogatory, the less it affects your scores. This is called "Aging Out." In my experience, derogatory accounts without balances (i.e. late pays, paid collections, paid public records, etc.) start noticeably aging out at 6 months, then again at 12 months, 18 months and 24 months. Keep in mind that derogatory accounts will affect your scores to some extent for as long as they are reported, however, as long as you are managing your credit wisely, they will age out over time.

---

6. **Number Of Past Due Items** - Along with the previous categories, this one deals with late or delinquent accounts by counting the number of accounts you have that are past due.

WORD OF CAUTION

In this factor, it is important to remember that all it takes is one derogatory mark to drop your credit scores by as much as 80-100 points. One recent late pay, one collection, one past due account.

---

7. **Number Of Accounts Paid As Agreed** – This is where good credit items count most. This category reports how many accounts you have paid on time, without any late or missed payments. It reports even closed accounts that were paid off as agreed.

Universal Default Defined

The points lost to a poor payment history can indeed be very damaging, but that's only the beginning of the problems that can arise from poor payment history. Those who pay late make themselves vulnerable to a devastating situation called Universal Default, which is basically the equivalent of every one of your creditors ganging up on you all at once and making your life a living hell.

Here's how it happens. Your existing creditors can legally conduct periodic checks on your credit. If they find you have missed a payment on any account, or that your scores have gone down, they consider it a breech, allowing them to raise your APR by a significant amount. Most often, a default APR is buried in the fine print when you apply for the credit card. This is the rate they will raise you to if they find you in breach of your credit contracts. This can be 28%, or even higher.

And that's not all. Universal Default can cause many creditors to close credit card accounts, causing you to have an account *closed by a creditor* with a balance, and in most instances creditors will immediately lower your credit card limits. As you learned in Chapter 7, this means that if you have balances on those credit cards the debt ratio to limit will be altered, forcing you into a situation where you find yourself losing up to 150 points for a handful of maxed out credit cards.

A universal default situation can be the catalyst for financial disaster. It is unfair. However, for now, this one is set in stone. For this reason, it is imperative that you stay on top of your payment history factor. The following tips will help.

Tips For Improving The Payment History Factor

1. **Verify the data being reported**. Here are some examples:

    a) Late Pays. As discussed above, late pays age out; however, any lates within the last 12-24 months not only affect your credit scores more severely but can also affect your ability to get a loan no matter how high your scores are. It depends on lender requirements.

    The tip here is that creditors are notorious for reporting late pays in the wrong month. This is because they are backlogged on data entry.

    If you have a late pay reporting, make sure that you check your records to confirm that it is being reported for the month that you were actually late. See the Real Life

Success Story at the end of this chapter.

b) Check for collections. There has been an explosion of nationwide collection scams that make it necessary for you to check your reports quarterly to ensure that you are not a victim of such a scam. According to the Fair Debt Collections Act (FDCA), the burden of proof is on the collector. If they cannot provide you with proof (which I will talk about in Chapter 18), the account must be deleted from your credit report.

c) Make sure that there are no past due amounts being listed. Sometimes creditors forget to update this part of your file.

d) Make sure you recognize all creditors and accounts being reported. Good and bad.

e) Make sure that your *good accounts* are being reported to all three credit bureaus.

f) Make sure that closed accounts are showing as closed without balances. As discussed in Chapter 7, there are many times when mortgage and auto accounts do not update to "closed and paid" for months—or even at all.

g) Make sure the Open Date, Date of Last Activity, and Close Date are accurate. And most importantly, the Date of Last Delinquency on negative accounts. Remember, the older a negative gets, the less it affects your score. But more importantly, as you will read in Chapter 14, the Statute of Limitations and the 7-Year Reporting Period are both triggered by this date. Collection agencies frequently re-date accounts, and when they do, it is a violation of all ACTS that are in place to protect consumers.

h) After making sure all dates are accurately recorded, check the Statute of Limitations in your state, and the 7-Year Reporting Period to see if derogatory items should be removed. Again, in Chapter 14, I list the current state statute of limitations. In many instances, the credit bureaus do not automatically remove expired derogatory accounts; therefore, it is up to you to request removal.

2. **Pay all of your accounts on time.** This is the factor you can take immediate control over to effectively manage your credit scores. Here are your options that make it easy to make sure your payments reach the creditor before the due date passes:

    a) I always suggest that my clients change their due dates to fit within their budget. If your finances do not allow for you to pay all of your bills on the 1st of each month, then set half of your bills up for the 1st, and the other half on the 15th. Most creditors will work with you to make these changes quickly.

    b) Make sure you know the grace periods on your accounts. Be aware that some creditors have no grace period and that if payment is not made by the due date on your statement, you will be considered 30 days late. In other instances, if the due date on the statement is June 1, you will have until June 29 before you are considered 30 days late. However, in this instance creditors will usually charge a late fee if payment isn't received by the 15th day.

    c) Set up a system to remind yourself to mail your payments at least 7-10 days before the due date so they will reach the creditor in a timely manner. For an alert system you can use your cell phone, your email account, or your electronic calendar.

    d) Pay your bills when you receive them. I understand that not everyone has cash flow to do this, but if you can it's a great way to make sure that you won't get hit with a late pay on your credit scores, especially if you constantly forget due dates.

    e) Online bill pay is a great way to manage your debt well. You can schedule automatic payments or log on and pay them manually as needed. However, it can take 3-5 days for online payments to clear, so be sure to leave yourself enough time. The date you submit payment is not considered the date paid. Date paid is when your payment clears.

f) Automatic withdraw is the easiest method if it is available through your creditors. This option allows the creditor to pull the payment from your checking account automatically on an agreed upon date each month.

CREDIT TIP

If you make your payments on the actual due date, be sure to do so via the telephone, *not online*. Also, be sure that you call in your payment before the cut-off time, which is usually 4:00PM EST. If you fail to do so, you risk being reported late.

---

3. When transitioning to a new mortgage loan, *don't count on escrow to pay the final mortgage payment* of a previous loan. Call the previous lender at least three days before the due date of the last payment and confirm that payment has been made. If not, pay it to be safe and keep all records so that you can collect the money back from the new escrow account.

    No matter how high your scores, a single 30-day mortgage late can cost you 80 points. It can take several months to earn back those points—precious time that you don't have when you are in the process of a new loan. Losing those points today can cost you tens, if not hundreds of thousands of dollars over the life of the loan.

4. Some creditors do not report until you are 60 days late. If you know that you are not going to be able to pay all of your credit card payments on time, call each creditor to find out whether or not they report at 30 or 60 days so that you can decide which cards to pay first.

5. If you should happen to forget or miss a payment, get back on top of things immediately. The sooner you get current on accounts the better off you'll be; if a late payment is reported, the time since a late payment is also reported. If you make future payments on time, you'll prevent the score from going down further.

6. There are times when you cannot manage your credit, whether because you have lost your job, are injured and unable to work, or

have just gotten in over your head. If this happens to you, contact your creditors. Frequently, they will negotiate different payment terms, lower your interest rate, or make some other arrangement to help you pay off your debt.

7. The best advice I can give you about the payment history portion of your score is to be proactive. It is easier to prevent credit problems than to erase them. If you are already managing your accounts by paying your bills on time, keep up the good work. There are other factors that influence your credit scores, but payment history is the largest and pulls the most weight of any of them.

Real Life Success Story: Marilyn

Marilyn had immaculate credit. That is, until she incurred a 30-day late on her mortgage payment. This caused her score to drop 80 points. The credit bureaus reported that the late payment occurred in January. Marilyn knew she wasn't late in January, but rather in December. So I phoned the creditor. And, without acknowledging Marilyn's December late pay, I explained that they mistakenly reported a 30-day late in January that had not occurred. I requested that they research it. They confirmed that Marilyn was not late in January. As a result, the creditor willingly faxed a letter to Marilyn *confirming their error*. Marilyn took the letter to her mortgage broker who had the report corrected, resulting in her score instantly shooting up 75 points. How could I accomplish this?

The law states that creditors and credit bureaus must remove inaccurately reported information. Yes, in this case, Marilyn had been late in paying her December mortgage; however, the report did not reflect this fact. Therefore, by law, the creditor had to purge it from her reports. That's why it is so important to verify all reported items on a derogatory account before conceding anything.

THE REAL DEAL

You have all heard the well-used phrase, "life happens." I regretfully tell you—your creditors and the three credit bureaus don't care. They hear hard luck and off beat stories all day, everyday. There is nothing that you can tell them that they haven't heard, and the end result will render you no better off than before you picked up the phone or sent the email.

Our fast paced lifestyles make it virtually inevitable that, absent a bullet-proof organizational system, you will fall behind if you are not careful. Your payment history accounts for the biggest percentage of your credit score. An incredible 35% of your score is controlled by how you keep you up with the payment of your bills. For this reason, it is incredibly important that you exhaust every remedy to make sure that you have an organized system you can live with for the long haul.

CHAPTER 9

The Five Factors Of Credit: Part Three - Length of History

15% Is Length of Credit History – Worth 127.5 Points

Among factors that go into making up your credit scores, length of credit history accounts for 15% and can generate as much as 127.5 points. That's a big percentage, and to maximize those points it's well worth making sure you manage your length of credit history wisely.

While each of the five credit score factors has its own importance, length of credit is highly significant because it traces your credit path all the way back to your oldest listed account. Logic tells you that the longer your credit history, the higher the score for this particular factor, right? Actually, wrong. New credit users–less than a year–can carry higher scores than seasoned users. This factor requires meticulous attention if you want to gain access to those 127.5 points.

What This Factor Considers

Your Length of Credit History is calculated by taking your oldest credit record on file and your most recent line of credit and calculating an average length of time for all of your credit.

Per Fair Isaac & Co., when calculating your credit scores, this factor considers the following:

1. **How long** your credit accounts have been in force. You receive

91

points based on the average length of your individual credit histories with each creditor.

2. **How long** you have held specific types of credit accounts.

3. **How long** it has been since you used certain accounts.

Based on my experience, there's a lot more to it than these three items that Fair Isaac & Co. indicates. The following tips provide some great insight and opportunity to make quick improvement in this segment of your credit report.

Tips For Improving The Length Of Credit History Factor

You cannot simply create a history out of thin air. But you can show potential creditors that you have a responsible credit history, even if it's a short one. Here are some tips for beefing up this part of your score:

1. **Make Sure You Get Credit For Credit.** One of the most important aspects about the Length of Credit History Factor is to make certain that all of your records are reflected in your credit report. As noted previously, not all creditors report to each of the three credit bureaus, so you may not be receiving all of your earned points.

   If you have good credit accounts that are not listed, write to the creditor and to the credit bureaus asking them to report the good accounts on your credit report. As you know, single points can make the difference when it comes to getting the best loan possible. If you have the history, you deserve the points.

2. **Don't Close Accounts.** Even if you have accounts that you haven't used for quite some time, don't close them. They still factor into your length of credit history. Many people have multiple lines of credit, but only use one or two cards. That's okay. It's far better to retain that history than to cut it off.

   Open accounts remain on your report indefinitely; however, if you close an account, it will fall off of your report in 7-10 years.

   I have seen hundreds of reports that show an old Sears or JC Penney account from the 1970s or 1980s. These reports generally come with very high credit scores.

The only exceptions would be in the case of divorce or identity theft.

3. **How And When To Add New Accounts.** Do not add new credit when you are thinking about entering into a loan transaction. New accounts will lower your overall account age and diminish your length of credit history for a period of 3-6 months, so be sure to have cushion in your score. Even if you've used credit for a very long time, opening a new account can lower your credit scores.

How many points will be lost depends on your overall credit profile, but the temporary loss is usually minimal. Even so, single points can make a huge difference in interest rates and fees.

4. **Open New Accounts Wisely.** Don't open a lot of new accounts at once. That strategy will also lower your average account age, negatively impacting your score.

5. **Make Sure Dates Are Reported Accurately.** Length of credit history depends on dates. Inaccurately reporting these dates is a common error in credit reports. Be sure to check the open dates on your accounts, and, if reported inaccurately, inform the credit bureaus that they need to be corrected.

6. **Personal Identification And Demographic Information.** Every time you fill out an application for credit, to rent an apartment, to apply for insurance, open a utility account, or open a bank account, that information gets sent to the credit bureaus. Just as there are errors in creditor information, there are also errors in your personal and demographic information, in the form of variations that come from data entry mistakes, inconsistency in filling out applications for credit, rentals, or purchases. What most consumers don't realize is that these errors take valuable points from their credit scores. Why? The more compilations of variations, the more it appears that you are not managing your credit, thus making you a credit risk. Think about it, if you were pulling your credit every 4-6 months, you would be cleaning up those variations. However, because most consumers don't check their credit reports until after they have been

denied for credit, these inconsistencies stack up, and the system penalizes consumers for not paying attention.

Here are some tips to assure that you don't lose points in this factor:

- Select one version of your name to be used from this day forward.

- Look for AKA's, other spellings or formats of your names. They should ALL be removed, every single variance with the exception of married, maiden or legally changed names. And in that case, there should only be one version of each name listed.

- Make sure that your current address is being reported accurately and in the same format to all three credit bureaus.

- Look for other addresses on your report. All credit reports have a section in which they list the addresses where you have lived. The problem is, in most instances, you will have too many, and that hurts your score. They should not be listing work or business addresses, or friends' addresses, or temporary addresses on your report. Limit the amount of addresses reporting to 3, no more than 5. Be sure to keep the oldest and most recent, and one in the middle for history purposes. All other variations, duplications and extra addresses should be removed.

- Check your Date of Birth across all three credit bureaus.

- Check your Employment History. Remove all history except for your oldest employment, and your current employment. Keep it down to no more than three.

- Check the Telephone Numbers being listed, if any. Remove all inactive numbers.

- Look for other social security numbers being reported on your report. Look everywhere. They could be hidden in the notes, or in an obvious place. You MUST remove all social security numbers that do not belong to you immediately. Even if they belong to your spouse, your child, or someone you know. However, prior to asking for removal, you want to be sure that the credit bureau has not crossed accounts with that social security number onto your report. If any listed accounts do not belong to you and there's a random social security number printed somewhere on your report, be sure that you list the accounts in the same letter that you send to the credit bureaus asking them to remove the random social security number. THIS IS NOT identity theft, it is an error. But it's still a problem.

The more variations compiled on your report the more points you are losing in this factor. I advise you to pull your credit report every 4-6 months from each of the credit bureaus to find and fix such errors. Going forward, be consistent in how you fill out credit applications. If you change your address, or you get married and change your name, make sure that the credit bureaus have the correct information.

Real Life Success Story: Joseph

Joseph was beyond frustrated when he came to me for help. He had recently applied for a home loan and learned that while his TransUnion and Equifax scores were in the 700s, Experian reported his score as being in the low 500s, listing several negative accounts that did not belong to him.

Three months of his sending letters and making phone calls to Experian got him nowhere, and left him completely frustrated and discouraged. No matter what proof he sent, Experian simply replied that they had "verified" the information with the creditors. After careful review of his report, I found a social security number hidden in the back pages that was just one digit off from Joseph's. Obviously, this misplaced social security number was the source of the errors that caused Joseph months of aggravation. A data entry person at the credit bureau made an error while entering Joseph's personal information.

I wrote one letter which contained the story, the drama–and some lawsuit references– and sent it to all creditors, certified, so that I could track delivery. I then sent a package to Experian which included a copy of every letter sent to the creditors with proof of delivery, a copy of Joseph's credit report with notes referencing all accounts that did not belong to him, and, of course, a copy of an important recent legal verdict which found one of the credit bureaus liable for compensatory damages of $106,000 in economic damages and $245,000 in punitive damages. That legal decision faulted the credit bureau for causing mental anguish through ineptitude and inaction. The jury found that they were in violation of the Fair Credit Reporting Act, which sets the requirements for credit reporting agencies to ensure they maintain accurate records on consumers.

It didn't happen overnight, but within a couple of months, Joseph's reports were back to normal.

THE REAL DEAL

Your Length of Credit History is an important aspect of your credit, accounting for 15% of your overall score. It's also a factor that you can improve by simply employing the knowledge you have gained from all of the chapters of this book so far. Your Length of Credit History is not a challenging factor; it is quite straightforward and easy to maximize once you put this valuable information to use. As long as you put good credit into action as early as you can, and navigate your credit course with the tips laid out here, you should have no trouble making the most of your length of credit history.

CHAPTER 10

The Five Factors Of Credit: Part Four - Mix of Credit

10% Is Mix of Credit – Worth 85 Points

The mix of your credit accounts for 10% of your credit score. What does this mean? The credit scoring system is programmed to analyze different types of consumer credit accounts. Consumers need to prove that they can manage multiple types of credit, each involving different rules and agreements.

This particular factor of the score is complex in its simplicity. On the one hand, the concept is very basic: maintain a good mix of high quality credit and handle each of those relationships well. Sounds easy enough, doesn't it? The complex part is knowing what kind of credit accounts are best for maximizing this factor, as well as knowing how much is sufficient. Understanding these relevant issues can help you add significant points to your credit history.

What This Factor Considers

Per Fair Isaac & Co., when calculating your score, this factor considers the following elements:

- Number of (presence, prevalence, and recent information on) various types of accounts

That's it? Not too much to go on, is it? Let me use my experience to explain what this means and how you can get those 85 points. First, let's take a look at some of the different types of accounts considered:

1. **Revolving Accounts** – Revolving accounts require a different payment each month with a percentage of the amount owed being the minimum payment. Examples of revolving accounts include:

    a) **Major Credit Card Accounts**: These include bank issued Visa and MasterCard's as well as non-bank-issued cards such as Discover and American Express.

    b) **Secured Credit Cards**: As discussed in Chapter 7, a secured credit card is like a secured loan wherein the consumer deposits money into a savings account as collateral for a line of credit. However, the card is considered the same as a major credit card when it comes to the credit scoring system.

    c) **Department Store And Gas Company Cards**: These are single purpose credit cards accepted only by the merchant who distributes them. As such, department store credit and gas cards are considered as low quality credit. The credit scoring system is programmed to grade consumers as desperate if they have to resort to a third-party for financing!

    d) **Home Equity Lines Of Credit (HELOC)**: Sometimes these types of accounts are reported to the credit bureaus as revolving accounts. NOT GOOD and unfair because, as we all know, this type of loan is secured by your home, right! The rule is very clear. If you max out a revolving account, your score can go down by 80 points. The reason most consumers get a HELOC is to remodel, refurnish, or consolidate debt. The bottom line is that they almost always max out a HELOC.

2. **Installment Accounts** – Installment accounts carry a fixed payment. Examples of installment accounts are auto loans, student loans, home equity loans, signature loans and fixed-rate mortgages.

3. **Open Accounts** – Open accounts have no limits and must be paid in full every month. Examples include, but are not limited to, American Express cards due in full every 30 days, utility bills, and cellular phone bills. My experience is that utility and cellular accounts

do not make a big impact on the score unless they become delinquent. If this happens the scores will go down.

The Perfect Mix Of Credit

There really is no standard perfect mix of credit, but here are some great guidelines based on where you are with your credit history.

- For new credit users (0-1 year): 1-2 major credit cards

- For semi new credit users (1-3 years): 2-3 major credit cards, and an auto loan

- For seasoned credit users (3-7 years): 2-3 major credit cards, an auto loan and a mortgage

- Anything beyond 7 years: As much good credit as you want!

Just like the perfect pot of minestrone, a little bit of something can add depth and interest, while too much can really detract from the overall mix. It's the same with credit. The reason it is so important to be picky about the lines of credit you establish is because once you open a line of credit, it is on your record for a very long time.

The key is to have as much high quality credit as possible, with a good blend of revolving and installment debt.

CREDIT TIP

Mortgages are considered higher-quality credit. Consumers with mortgages are perceived to have much to protect when it comes to their credit and their debt obligations. They have an incentive to pay their bills on time.

By understanding how the scoring system looks at each type of credit and the amount of the type of credit you have, you can improve your score. In Chapters 7 and 8, I've given a wealth of information and tips on several areas that affect your Mix of Credit, including:

- Having open credit card accounts.

- Making sure all good credit is being reported to all three credit bureaus.

- Avoiding third-party financing (i.e. department store credit cards)

Here are a few more tips to help you make the most of the 85 points allocated to this factor of your credit scores.

Tips For Improving The Mix Of Credit Factor

1. Opening new credit accounts temporarily lowers your scores in two ways. First, you will lose points for having a hard inquiry. Second, you will lose points for the new debt. The good news is that after 2-3 months of paying the new account on time, your scores will go back up since you've demonstrated that you can manage your new credit as part of your overall credit mix.

    This is why I advise my clients to never apply for credit if they are planning to enter into a loan transaction in the near future, or if they are in the middle of a home loan transaction.

2. If you are in a position of needing to open a couple of credit card accounts, you should either open them within a few days of each other, or at least 60-90 days apart. The credit scoring system is easily manipulated, and if it sees that you are opening multiple credit accounts in a short period of time you will appear to be in financial trouble, and you will be red flagged.

3. If you have a HELOC showing as a revolving account, write to the credit bureaus and ask them to change it to "Installment" or "Other." If they don't make the change the first time, try again. You will eventually prevail and your credit scores will show the reward immediately.

4. Don't apply for too many credit cards. Follow the guidelines I've outlined above. A little credit used prudently demonstrates a proven track record; too many lines of credit can make you look like a kid in a candy store.

5. Because most American Express cards are considered open accounts, it's best not to rely on this type of card to establish new credit or to fulfill the requirements of mix of credit as outlined above.

6. Auto Financing is a great way to prove your credit worthiness and

will help your mix of credit. So avoid paying cash for a car at all times if you can. If you do not have an auto loan on your profile, and cannot get an auto loan at this time, a co-signed loan is always a good option.

THE REAL DEAL

Your mix of credit is an important factor that goes into your overall credit scores. Generally speaking mix of credit is not a big determiner of whether or not you will get credit, but it can certainly help you achieve *better* credit. And, with the hurdles being raised ever higher for consumers to improve their scores to gain loans, it is certainly well worth focusing on every point. The types of credit you have, the quality of that credit, the timing of how you go about adding new credit, all go into generating the score in this factor: creating your credit mix.

Choose your avenues of credit carefully, both in the types of credit you carry and in the amount of credit of any one type that you carry. In doing so, you will be able to maintain the highest credit score possible in this factor. It's also important to know that credit scoring does not make an infallible decision about you and your creditworthiness. Each lender will look at you differently and weigh the considerations individually. For this reason, it's very important to give the impression of being a very good manager of your credit. The right mix of credit will help you look better in the eyes of the lenders.

CHAPTER 11

The Five Factors Of Credit: Part Five - Inquiries

10% Is New Credit (aka: Inquiries) - Worth 85 Points

Consumers are bombarded daily with new credit offers! It seems that everywhere they turn someone is advertising a "special offer" for a new credit card, a new interest rate, or even a new spending limit. These days it's gotten so bad that you can't go to the mall, a department store, or to your own mailboxes without someone asking you to apply for an additional line of credit.

Regardless of why you respond to a credit offer, the holidays, an emergency, a great sounding offer, you should always be aware that credit card companies will immediately run a credit inquiry which may cause you, depending on your circumstances, to lose between one and 20 points from your score.

According to Fair Isaac & Co., the process of applying for new credit makes up 10% of your credit scores. There are two types of inquiries that you need to know about. Here's the difference:

Soft Inquiry

Soft inquiries DO NOT affect your credit scores. Here are some examples of what would be considered soft inquiries:

- When *you* pull your own credit.

- When one of your existing creditors does a periodic review of your credit. This is called an *account review*.

- When a creditor has purchased your name from the credit bureaus for the purposes of sending you some sort of credit solicitation in the mail. This is called a *promotional inquiry*.

- When an employer checks your credit before hiring you.

- When you apply for auto insurance.

- When a landlord checks your credit.

Hard Inquiry

Hard inquiries DO affect your score. A hard inquiry occurs when you apply for a loan, a credit card, or any type of credit. Here are some examples of what can cause a hard inquiry to show up on your credit report:

- When you apply for a mortgage or home equity line of credit.

- When you apply for an auto loan.

- When you apply for a credit card.

- When you apply for a student loan.

- When you fill out and return pre-approved credit offers that you receive in the mail.

- When you apply for instant credit offers at the shopping mall.

- When you apply for credit on the internet.

- When you opt to become pre-qualified for any type of loan.

What This Factor Considers

You may be wondering why this information matters to your credit scores. From a creditor's point of view, consumers who have excessively shopped for credit in the past 6-12 months may be *trying to spend beyond their means, making them* a higher credit risk than consumers who have not.

Statistical studies also show that multiple inquiries can often be associated with a high risk of default, since distressed borrowers desperate for assistance are known to contact many lenders in hopes of finding someone who will approve them whether they can afford the new credit line or not.

De-Duplication – Mortgage and Auto Inquiries

Fair Isaac & Co. determined that a consumer shouldn't be punished for something as logical as shopping around for the best interest rates before buying a car or home, so they came up with something called De-Duplication. This means that you can have your credit pulled by as many mortgage or auto lenders as you want within a specified period of time and it will only be counted as one hard inquiry against your credit scores. And even better, provided the inquiries are coded correctly, auto and mortgage related inquiries that occur 30 days prior to scoring have no effect on the score. This is called a 30-day buffer.

The specified period of time depends on what version of the scoring software the lender is using to pull your credit reports and scores. As outlined in Chapter 5, if they are using the older version (Beacon-Classic FICO), then the de-duplication window is 14 days. If they are using the updated version (NextGen 2.0), then the de-duplication window is 45 days. Although Next-Gen 2.0 was rolled out a few years ago, there is no guarantee that all credit score vendors are using this model that allows 45 days of shopping to be considered as one hard inquiry. On the other hand, since the Beacon model was the first version of FICO on the market, consumers can feel safe in using the original 14-day window as a guideline. And I will use the 14-day window in the following example:

This is how it works. You go to an auto lender on February 1, and they pull your credit. The scores that they pull will not consider auto loan inquiries made by you between January 1 and January 30 as hard inquires. However, any auto inquires made before January 1 will be considered. This is your 30-day buffer.

So, in this example, you have from February 1 to February 14 to apply for as many auto loans as you want and they will be considered as one hard inquiry to your credit scores. However, you will lose points for the initial inquiry on February 1, and those points will not be deducted until the next time you have your credit pulled. So on February 2, your score may be a few points lower.

Let's say that you do not find a car by February 14, and you apply again on February 15, the 14-day de-duplication period will start again, and you will be hit with another hard inquiry.

The following tips will help you make sure that you keep your score in this factor as high as you can:

Tips For Improving The New Credit Factor

1. Hard inquiries will remain on your report for 2 years, and will affect your score for 1 year. If you see an inquiry on your report that you did not sign for, seek removal immediately by writing a letter to the creditor and the credit bureaus putting them on notice that you did NOT authorize the inquiry. This factor falls under the same consumer protection laws as all other factors; meaning, the creditors and credit bureaus are held to a standard of making sure the information they are reporting is true and accurate.

2. Hard Inquiries can cost anywhere between one and 20 points. It all depends on how the rest of your factors are being managed. If you have a credit score below 620, an inquiry will cost you more points than someone with a 720 score.

3. Good news. Multiple auto or mortgage inquiries in any 14-day period are counted as only one inquiry. Don't start shopping until you are prepared to make a purchase. This way you will avoid unnecessary dings to your credit scores.

4. Bad news. The credit scoring system does not like third-party credit card inquiries, so avoid discount offers from department stores.

5. Keep in mind that when you receive unsolicited mail that says, "You are Pre-Approved," it does NOT mean you are pre-approved. To be safe, stay away from these types of credit offers.

6. You should always check your credit reports and scores prior to shopping for loans or any type of credit. First, you will know whether or not you are credit ready to shop; and second, if you know what your credit scores are when you go out shopping, you can ask lenders and creditors whether or not you will qualify for their product, prior to them pulling your credit reports, resulting in a loss of points for a hard inquiry.

THE REAL DEAL

It is critical for all of us to understand every aspect of our credit report. As you now know, new credit accounts for 10% of your credit score, and hard inquiries, which you now understand, are considered a component of the new credit quotient. Although only 10%, it can become a very big deal. A huge deal if it prevents you from obtaining the credit you need. If you don't remember anything else, please remember that credit inquiries always impact your bottom line. Do the things that are necessary to enhance your future and financial wellbeing. By managing this important factor, you'll be one step closer to earning the credit you need and desire.

CHAPTER 12

Forget What You Think You Know About Credit

Some of the most devastating credit mistakes I have witnessed come from individuals who followed bad advice by falling prey to credit myths. They read articles, bought books, or followed the well meaning, but misguided advice of family, co-workers, friends, and financial gurus. The information they received sounded good, and seemed sensible, but it was dead wrong and it cost them big.

The credit system can seem peculiar because an action can seem to make total sense and still be wrong. So, this chapter highlights the top 20 credit myths that cause even credit conscientious consumers to falter. You have seen much of this information in other areas of the book, but I believe it's important to have these top 20 credit myths in one place for easy reference.

This important chapter will help you improve your chances of long-term credit success and avoid the traps of dangerous credit mistakes.

20 POWERFUL CREDIT MYTHS

Myth 1 – You Should Avoid Using Credit Cards

How many times have you heard people on syndicated television or radio advise consumers to cut up their credit cards and pay everything with cash as part of a financial plan? This advice is counterproductive when it comes to the credit scoring system.

Now that you know that 30% of your credit scores is made up of how you use and manage your credit card accounts and debt, I hope you will agree with my conclusion that an all cash plan may be a good way to get rid of debt, but it's utter destruction to your credit scores.

Myth 2 – The Amount Of The Credit Card Limit Makes A Difference

The amount of your credit card limit does NOT make a difference to the credit scoring system. The important number is the ratio between the balance (debt owed) and the allowable spending limit. The scoring system sees no difference between a $5 limit and a $50,000 limit. If you have a $4.99 balance on a $5 card, you will be penalized the same as if it were $49,999 on a $50,000 card. It's all about the percentage spent in relation to the amount allowed.

Myth 3 – Consolidating Debt Onto A Low-Interest Credit Card Will Increase Your Scores

Dig yourself out of your financial hole with a balance transfer. Credit card companies tempt you with big checks, personalized with your name already printed on them. Take a vacation. Improve your home. These checks are yours to do whatever you want.

Sounds great, doesn't it? And it would be great except that if you consolidate all of your debt onto one credit card, you will max out that card and your credit scores will drop 80-100 points overnight! Oops, they forgot to tell you that! And then, all of your credit card interest rates, including theirs, will increase to the highest amount allowed, making it almost impossible for you to pay your balances down.

Myth 4 – You Have To Keep A Balance On Your Credit Card Or The Card Won't Be Rated

As long as you use your credit cards, you will be rated. Revolving accounts become unrated due to the *lack of use*, not whether or not there is a balance. So, if you have credit cards, it's best not to allow them to become dormant.

Myth 5 – It's Okay If You Go Over Your Credit Card Limit Because The Credit Card Company Authorized The Purchase

Nothing is further from the truth. Don't go over your credit card limits, even if it's just by one dollar. As I wrote in Chapter 7, doing so deals you a double penalty and you could lose 80-100 points from your scores if you have the points to lose.

Myth 6 – Closing Credit Card Accounts Will Help Your Score

I promise I'll only say it one more time! Don't close credit card accounts at all, with the following exceptions: closing a joint account after a divorce; removing your name from an authorized user account that has incurred negative history or has high balance-to-limit ratios; or in the case of identity theft.

You will lose points in two factors when you close a credit card account, both in the Amounts Owed Factor which is worth 30% of your credit score, and in the Length of Credit History Factor which is worth 15% of your credit score.

Myth 7 – As Long As You Pay Off Your Credit Card Balance Every Month, Your Score Will Go Up

Many of my clients have made the mistake of thinking that as long as they pay their bills on time, their scores should improve, but that isn't the case if you carry high balances. The balance that hits your statement each month is the balance that gets reported to the credit bureaus. This is the balance that will be calculated in your credit scores. And now you know the rules. If the balance on your credit cards is over 50% of its limit when your statement is printed, you are losing points. I advise my clients to get into the habit of paying your statements before they are due. (See Chapter 7.)

Myth 8 – Using Debit/ATM Cards Will Help Build Or Rebuild Your Credit Scores

With increasing frequency, consumers will swipe their debit cards at the grocery store or at the mall. They mistakenly believe that using a bank debit card instead of a credit card will somehow improve their credit scores. This is not true. Although these cards are labeled Visa and MasterCard, debit cards are the same as cash. Using a debit card does nothing to enhance your credit scores.

Myth 9 – The Type Of Credit Card Doesn't Matter

We talked about this in Chapter 10. The credit scoring system does not like third-party finance cards (i.e., department store cards, furniture store cards, gas cards.) It appears that consumers are desperate if they cannot obtain a major credit card. Always try to use major credit cards offered through major financial institutions that report to all three credit bureaus every 30 days.

Myth 10 – Those Pre-Approved Credit Card Offers Do Not Hurt Your Score

Just because credit is offered to you, it does not mean that you should accept it. When you receive a pre-approved credit card letter in the mail, your credit report has not been pulled yet, so you are NOT approved for the account.

Myth 11 – Paying Off An Old Collection Or Charge-Off Will Increase Your Credit Scores

This myth is surrounded by controversy, mostly because many people don't understand the true effect that paying off old collection accounts has on credit scores. If you have a collection account and you make payment on it, or make a written or oral promise to pay it, you risk an immediate drop in your credit scores, and also risk renewing the statute of limitations on the account. I talk about this in great detail in Chapters 14 and 18.

Myth 12 – The Credit Bureaus Have 30 Days To Respond To A Dispute Or They Have To Delete The Items From My Reports

I wish it was that easy. This is one of the most common misconceptions I hear from clients when they contact me for help. Basically, the consumer credit protection laws lay out specific time guidelines in which credit bureaus must respond to a consumer's dispute. Yes, they have 30 days to respond; however, you have to allow for mail delivery time to and from, meaning that 30 days has now become 40-45 days.

On top of that, the credit bureaus use stall tactics. They will either send a letter telling you that they've received your dispute and will give you a date in the near future that they will respond to your dispute, or they will send you a stall tactic letter asking for copies of your proof of social security, even if you've already sent it. The bottom line is that it could take more than 60 days to receive a first response to your dispute.

Myth 13 – If I Get One Credit Bureau To Remove An Account, They Will All Remove It Automatically

The credit bureaus do NOT work with each other. They are competitors and do not share data. You must contact each credit bureau individually to make sure that negative or incorrect items are deleted or removed.

Myth 14 – Your Divorce Decree Protects Your Credit Scores

The agreement with the creditor takes precedence over the divorce decree. So if you are a joint owner of an account, you are responsible for the debt, regardless of what the judge says. I will talk about this more in Chapter 20.

Myth 15 – Marrying Someone Who Has Poor Credit Will Hurt Your Credit Scores

Although getting married generally means that you'll be combining finances, it does not mean that your credit will be combined. As a matter of fact, the only time the same account should show up on both reports is when you have opened a joint account together, co-signed for each other, or added your spouse as an authorized user on a credit card account. Old history, good and bad, cannot legally be reported on your spouse's credit report if they did not sign as a joint owner.

WORD OF CAUTION

If you and your spouse have a joint account and you are entering into a dispute with the credit bureaus, you MUST dispute separately. Even if the credit bureau removes a negative item from one spouse's report, this does not mean that they will remove it from the other, unless you have documented proof supporting your claim.

Myth 16 – Paying Or Settling A Negative Account Such As A Judgment, Lien, Or Charge-Off Will Remove That Item From Your Credit Reports

Many people think that if they pay off a negative account, it will be removed from their credit reports or will immediately improve their credit scores. This is not the case. There are specific statutes that allow these items to remain on the reports. However, that does not mean that you cannot seek early removal.

Myth 17 – Derogatory Credit Will Automatically Drop Off Of Your Credit Report After Seven Years!

Sometimes it does and sometimes it doesn't. It's always best to make sure that you keep track of the dates when items should be removed. And then follow up with the credit bureaus to make sure it happens.

Myth 18 – Mortgage Lenders Use The Average Of My Three Credit Scores

Mortgage lenders do not blend credit scores. When they receive all three of your scores, they will use the middle score. Additionally, if you are applying jointly for a mortgage, in many instances they will use the lowest middle score of the two borrowers.

Myth 19 – If I Co-Sign For Someone, It Won't Affect My Credit

In the eyes of the credit bureaus, co-signing for an individual is essentially the same as applying for credit in your own name. You are agreeing to step up to take on the financial burden if that person fails to make payments. You should carefully consider the individuals you would be willing to co-sign for, as you have very little control over their ability to pay. On the other hand, their actions hold substantial control over YOUR credit.

I always advise my clients who are co-signing for their children to log into the account every month to make sure that the account is being paid on time. Remember, it only takes one 30-day late to drop your scores by 80 points.

Myth 20 – Your Salary Makes A Difference In Your Scores

While your salary is considered when it comes to a loan application, it has no bearing on your credit scores. The credit scoring system doesn't care if you make a lot of money or very little money. The real issue is whether you pay your bills on time, honor your cardholder and loan agreements, and manage your credit wisely. So you can make hundreds of thousands of dollars per year, but if your credit scores are low, you will pay penalty fees and higher interest rates, the same as anyone else with low credit scores. You will also face the real possibility of being denied credit.

And A Final Myth For Good Luck – Adding A Consumer Statement To Your Credit Reports Makes A Difference

A consumer statement is a personal statement that the Fair Credit Reporting Act allows you to add to your credit report telling your story behind a negative account. When a creditor or lender looks at your report, they will see the statement and should take it into consideration when making their credit decisions.

Unfortunately, when it comes to credit scores, a statement is nothing but text. Most lenders don't bother to read the text anymore. All they look at is the score, and whether or not there are public records or unpaid collections.

THE REAL DEAL

In today's rapid-fire age of information, bloggers, self-promotion and veiled advertisements, consumers have to carefully weigh the quality of advice they receive. Be warned, bad information often comes from very big sources. As a credit expert, these 20 myths reveal just a comprehensive handful of the advice and misinformation that leads consumers down a dangerous, destructive and false path.

The credit scoring system doesn't always make sense, and that really doesn't matter to you. What does matter is that you know the truth about credit scores and you know the right steps to take to improve and maintain a healthy credit rating.

CHAPTER 13

Your Rights
The Laws You Need
To Know To Win

The players in the credit industry hold information that has master power over your financial future. These companies manage hundreds of millions of files. Technology continues to advance, but the credit bureaus, creditors and collection agencies still make huge mistakes. Well, everyone make mistakes, but the trouble with these companies is that they sometimes stubbornly cling to their records, not budging from the position that they are right and you are wrong. However, in many instances, they are very wrong. The good news is that when they refuse to rectify their mistakes, there are laws that help consumers get a fair deal.

Can You Sue The Big Three And Win?

If you've ever been involved in a lawsuit, you know very well the high toll it takes on your life. Lawsuits are expensive, time-consuming, aggravating, emotionally trying, and draining on every one of your financial and emotional resources. Having said that, sometimes they are also unavoidable.

The very thought of taking on one of the monster sized credit bureaus or creditors is intimidating. They are big corporate entities that have high priced lawyers. However, if they are wrong, and you know they are wrong, you have a right to fight for yourself, and you have the right to win and win big!

Here's a handful of lawsuits brought by people who took on the big three and prevailed:

- ## Williams Vs. Equifax (Case No. 1:2007cv21353)

  In 2007, 37 year old Angela Williams finally got her name back, and a big award to go with it. Williams took suit against Equifax, Inc. for repeatedly violating federal credit reporting laws when they continually confused her with another person and reported to potential creditors that she was a bad credit risk. Williams alleged that Equifax passed along false information that made it impossible for her to get credit. She couldn't get credit cards, and she couldn't get a student loan. As a result, Williams was unable to pursue a license critical to her career. Prior to filing suit, Williams exhausted all of her non-court options; she sent her picture identification, Social Security number, all documentation to prove that she was who she said she was. The judge concluded that Equifax's sloppy business practices reached a punitive nature for Williams, and awarded her $219,000 in actual damages and $2.7 million in punitive damages. Now she can go get that license—if she still wants to, that is. Read more at http://www.news4jax.com/news/14776180/detail.html.

- ## Cortez Vs. TransUnion (Civ. No. 05-5684)

  In April 2007, a federal court jury in the U.S. District Court in Pennsylvania handed over an $800,000 verdict against TransUnion in a fair credit reporting case. The jury found that TransUnion reported mixed information belonging to a suspected narcotics trafficker on a consumer (plaintiff Sandra Cortez's) credit report, and failed to fix the error despite several disputes. The jury awarded $50,000 in emotional distress damages, and $750,000 in punitive damages.

  The jury determined that TransUnion had violated four provisions of the Fair Credit Reporting Act: 1) they did not conduct an initial investigation; 2) they failed to make proper disclosures to Cortez when she complained; 3) they did not note her dispute in subsequent reports; 4) they had no procedures to ensure "maximum possible accuracy" in their reports. Read more at http://news.findlaw.com/andrews/bt/prv/20070508/20070508_cortez.html.

- ## Sloan Vs. Equifax, Experian & TransUnion (No. 1:05-CV-1272, (E.D. Va.)

In July 2006 a jury ordered Equifax to pay Suzanne Sloan, an identity theft victim, $351,000 over erroneous information that kept appearing on her credit report. Sloan had her Social Security number stolen by a hospital employee while giving birth to her child in 2003. The employee used it to open numerous accounts and ran up huge debts. Even though the thief was arrested in March 2004 and was sentenced to two years in prison, the victim spent two more years trying to clear up her credit.

"She wrote letters. She called them. They saw the problem. They just didn't fix it," said Blankingship of Blankingship & Associates in Alexandria, Va., Sloan's attorneys.

Sloan filed suits against all three credit bureaus. Experian and TransUnion settled, but Equifax fought to the end, and lost. Read more at http://news.technology.findlaw.com/andrews/bt/prv/20080115/20080115_sloane.html.

- ## Thomas Vs. TransUnion (Case No. 00-1150-Je)

In 2002, Judy Thomas was initially awarded $5.3 million in a federal case against TransUnion (later reduced to $1 million), found liable for willfully violating the federal Fair Credit Reporting Act, designed to ensure that credit companies provide accurate records and promptly correct mistakes.

Since 1996, TransUnion had listed the bad debts of Judith L. Upton of Washington on Thomas' credit reports. Both women have the same birth year, and similar first names. Their social security numbers differ by one digit.

Thomas spent seven years trying to rectify the situation on her own. She made TransUnion aware of the confusion. She called TransUnion, faxed, sent them documentation, sent them letters from the creditors corroborating that she was not the person that was credited. Thomas felt she was at war, and decided there would be no resolution without taking them to court. Read more at http://

www.cbsnews.com/stories/2002/07/31/earlyshow/living/money/
main517098.shtml.

Creditors And Collection Agencies Can Also Be Found At Fault

In addition to having the right to sue the Big Three, if you feel you have been wronged, you also have the right to sue obstinate creditors and collection agencies. In fact, such lawsuits crop up almost on a daily basis. The Internet is a powerful resource for researching past and existing lawsuits filed by consumers.

Certainly you will be able to locate a handful, if not hundreds of cases that will be very similar in nature to your complaint. By identifying cases similar to yours, you will gain an awareness of the viability of your case. Additionally, by conducting this type of research, and by focusing on your geographic region, you will also locate the names of lawyers who may be able to help you take on your adversary.

When The Law Is On Your Side

There are a ton of rules on the books that enable us to achieve fairness with regard to the credit bureaus, creditors and collection agencies. In many cases, citing the rules can help you to get the credit bureaus to make the necessary changes to your reports. It lets them know that you are well aware of your consumer rights and that you will not allow them to give you the runaround.

When seeking out the laws to help you make an impression, you don't have to learn them all. In fact, you would have to become a credit expert to understand the entire credit code. That is time-consuming and an oppressive burden that won't leave you much time for having a real life. So, here is a snapshot of the laws that can help you take on the credit industry and win.

The following summaries, where noted, are extracted in their entirety from The Federal Trade Commission's (FTC) website at http://www.ftc.gov. The FTC is the governing body of the U.S. government that oversees consumer trade activities. The FTC is there to protect consumers against fraudulent or unfair transactions. The information from the FTC is the final word on the laws and is the most up-to-date information consumers have on the important laws that are placed there for your protection. Additionally, supplemental content is also provided herein courtesy of http://www.white-house.gov fact sheets.

The U.S. Code And The Consumer Credit Protection Act Of 1968

The original legislation put into place that governs the credit industry is The United States Code (U.S. Code.) The U.S. Code is a compilation of all current United States law.

Under Title 15 of the U.S. Code (Commerce and Trade), in Chapter 41 you will find The Consumer Credit Protection Act of 1968. Considered to be landmark legislation, this Act is the most powerful tool consumers have to protect their credit reports and scores.

Since 1968, credit protections have multiplied rapidly. The concepts of "fair" and "equal" credit have been written into laws that bar unfair discrimination in credit transactions, require that consumers be told the reason when credit is denied, let borrowers find out about their credit records, and set up a way for consumers to settle billing disputes.

Each law was meant to reduce the problems and confusion about consumer credit, which as it became more widely used in our economy, also grew more complex. Together, these laws set a standard for how individuals are to be treated in their financial dealings.

It is important to know your rights and how to use them. I recommend that if you have a need or have any intention of entering into a legal process against a creditor, collection agency or credit bureau, that you set some time aside to read the full content of the consumer credit protection laws outlined below.

What To Do If You Believe That Your Rights Have Been Violated

If you believe that your rights have been violated, there are many laws that are there to protect you. In this chapter I have compiled a comprehensive listing of the laws that will help you protect yourself when you become involved in a credit industry battle. The following three actions should be taken in all instances of violation to commence a paper trail on the entity you are accusing. However, there are also specific actions that should be taken for certain ACTS, so please keep an eye out for these additional action tips throughout this section.

1. File a formal complaint with The Federal Trade Commission (FTC). The FTC works for the consumer to prevent fraudulent, deceptive, and unfair business practices in the marketplace. Although the FTC will not file a lawsuit on your behalf, they will start an investigation to help determine whether or not there has in fact been a violation.

   To file a complaint you can call 1-877-FTC-HELP or use the complaint form on their website at http://www.ftc.gov. You can also send your complaint to Consumer Response Center, Room 130, 600 Pennsylvania Avenue, N.W., Washington, D.C. 20580.

2. File a formal complaint with your State Attorney General's office. Many states have their own debt collection laws. Your Attorney General's office will give you access to that information.

3. Consider hiring a Consumer Credit attorney to help. Above, I give you examples of lawsuits that have been filed and won by consumers who had exhausted all efforts of protecting their rights on their own.

   To find a consumer credit attorney, I recommend cutting to the chase by searching out successful lawsuits on the internet, then contacting the counsel who handled each case. Send him or her your story, all documented proof, and the counsel may even take your case on contingency. No harm in asking.

A Summary Of The Rights That Protect You

The Fair Credit Reporting Act (FCRA) - 15 U.S.C. § 1681[1]

The federal Fair Credit Reporting Act (FCRA) promotes the accuracy, fairness, and privacy of information in the files of consumer reporting agencies. Consumer reporting agencies include the credit bureaus and specialty agencies (such as agencies that sell information about check writing histories, medical records, and rental history records). Here is a summary of your major rights under the FCRA.

1. You must be told if information in your file has been used against you. Anyone who uses a credit report or another type of consumer report to deny your application for credit, insurance, or employment—or to take another adverse action against you—must tell you, and must give you the name, address, and phone number of the agency that provided the information.

2. You have the right to know what is in your file. You may request and obtain all of the information about you in the files of a consumer reporting agency (your "file disclosure"). You are entitled to a free file disclosure if:

    a) a person has taken adverse action against you because of information in your credit report;

    b) you are the victim of identify theft and place a fraud alert in your file;

    c) your file contains inaccurate information as a result of fraud;

    d) you are on public assistance;

    e) you are unemployed but expect to apply for employment within 60 days.

    In addition, as of September 2005 all consumers are entitled to one free disclosure every 12 months upon request from each of the three credit bureaus, Equifax, Experian, and TransUnion.

3. You have the right to ask for a credit score from consumer reporting agencies.

4. You have the right to dispute incomplete or inaccurate information.

5. Consumer reporting agencies must correct or delete inaccurate, incomplete, or unverifiable information. Inaccurate, incomplete or unverifiable information must be removed or corrected. However, a consumer reporting agency may continue to report information it has verified as accurate.

6. Consumer reporting agencies may not report outdated negative in-formation.

7. Access to your file is limited. A consumer reporting agency may provide information about you only to people with a valid need–usually to consider an application with a creditor, insurer, employer, landlord, or other business. The FCRA specifies those with a valid need for access.

8. You must give your consent for reports to be provided to employers. A consumer reporting agency may not give out information about you to your employer, or a potential employer, without your written consent given to the employer.

9. You may limit "pre-screened" offers of credit and insurance you get based on information in your credit report. Unsolicited "prescreened" offers for credit and insurance must include a toll-free phone number you can call if you choose to remove your name and address from the lists these offers are based on. You may opt out with the nationwide credit bureaus at 1-888-5-OPTOUT (1-888-567-8688).

10. You may seek damages from violators. If a consumer reporting agency, or, in some cases, a user of consumer reports or a furnisher of information to a consumer reporting agency violates the FCRA, you may be able to sue in state or federal court.

11. Identity theft victims and active duty military personnel have ad-ditional rights.

States may enforce the FCRA, and many states have their own consumer reporting laws. For more information, including information about addition-al rights, go to http://www.ftc.gov/credit or write to: Consumer Response Center, Room 130-A, Federal Trade Commission, 600 Pennsylvania Ave. N.W., Washington, D.C. 20580.

What To Do If You Believe Your Rights Have Been Violated Under This Act

When faced with a potential Fair Credit Reporting Act case, the law provides a 2-year statute of limitations commencing from the date of the violation of the Act, regardless of whether the victim knows of the violation.

Violations of the FCRA can lead to both civil and criminal penalties. Civil penalties, include nominal damages (up to $1000 if no actual damages exist), actual damages (including emotional distress), and punitive damages, plus attorneys' fees and costs, may apply where there is "willful noncompliance" with the Act. Civil penalties for "negligent noncompliance" are restricted to actual damages and attorneys' fees and costs. Criminal penalties may apply where an individual knowingly and willfully obtains information from a consumer

The Fair And Accurate Credit Transactions Act (FACTA) – Public Law 108-159 [1]

On December 4, 2003, President Bush signed into law the Fair and Accurate Credit Transactions Act of 2003, as an amendment to the Fair Credit Reporting Act, to ensure that all citizens are treated fairly when they apply for a mortgage or other form of credit.

The legislation provides consumers, companies, consumer reporting agencies, and regulators with important new tools that expand access to credit and other financial services for all Americans, enhance the accuracy of consumers' financial information, and help fight identity theft.

Following are key amendments that have been put into place to help ensure that all Americans, of every income level and background, are able to build good credit and confront the problem of identify theft:

1. It ensures that lenders make decisions on loans based on full and fair credit histories, and not on discriminatory stereotypes.

2. It improves the quality of credit information, and protection for consumers against identity theft by:

   a) Giving every consumer the right to a copy of his or her credit report free of charge every year.

   b) Helping prevent identity theft before it occurs by requiring merchants to leave all but the last five digits of a credit card number off store receipts.

   c) Creating a national system of fraud detection to make identity thieves more likely to be caught. Previously, victims would have to make phone calls to all of their credit card companies and three major credit reporting agencies to alert them to the crime. Now consumers only need to make one call to receive advice, set off a nationwide fraud alert, and protect their credit standing.

d) Establishing a nationwide system of fraud alerts for consumers to place on their credit files. Credit reporting agencies that receive such alerts from consumers are obliged to follow procedures to ensure that any future requests are by the true consumer, not an identity thief posing as the consumer. The law also enables active duty military personnel to place special alerts on their files when they are deployed overseas.

e) Requiring regulators to devise a list of red flag indicators of identity theft, drawn from the patterns and practices of identity thieves.

f) Requiring lenders and credit reporting agencies to take action before a victim even knows a crime has occurred by drawing up a set of guidelines to identify patterns common to identity theft, and by developing methods to stop identity theft before it can cause major damage.

This legislation gives consumers unprecedented tools to fight identity theft and continued access to the most dynamic credit markets in the world. With a free credit report and powerful new tools to fight fraud, consumers have the ability to better protect themselves and their families.

The Equal Credit Opportunity Act (ECOA) - 15 U.S.C. § 1691 - 1691e[2]

The Equal Credit Opportunity Act (ECOA) ensures that all consumers are treated fairly when it comes to their chances to obtain credit. This does not mean that all consumers who apply for credit will get it. Factors such as income, expenses, debt, and credit history are considerations for creditworthiness. Not race or religion.

The law protects you when you deal with a creditor who regularly extends credit, including banks, small loan and finance companies, retail and department stores, credit card companies, and credit unions. Anyone involved in granting credit, such as real estate brokers who arrange financing, is covered under this law.

When You Apply For Credit, A Creditor May Not:

1. Consider, ask you to reveal or discourage you from applying based on your sex, marital status, age, race, national origin, or because you receive public assistance income. A creditor may ask you to voluntarily disclose this information (except for religion) but they cannot require it.

2. Ask if you're widowed or divorced. When permitted to ask marital status, a creditor may only use the terms: married, unmarried, or separated.

3. Ask about your marital status if you're applying for a separate, unsecured account. A creditor may ask you to provide this information if you live in "community property" states, including Arizona, California, Idaho, Louisiana, Nevada, New Mexico, Texas, and Washington.

4. Request information about your spouse, except when your spouse is applying with you; your spouse will be allowed to use the account; you are relying on your spouse's income or on alimony or child support income from a former spouse; or if you reside in a community property state.

5. Inquire about your plans for having or raising children.

6. Ask if you receive alimony, child support, or separate maintenance payments, unless they first advise you that you do not have to provide this information if you won't rely on these payments to get credit. A creditor may ask if you have to pay alimony, child support, or separate maintenance payments.

7. Consider whether you have a telephone listing in your name. A creditor may consider whether you have a phone.

8. Consider the race of people in the neighborhood where you want to buy, refinance or improve a house with borrowed money.

9. Consider your age, unless:

   a) you're too young to sign contracts, generally younger than 18 years of age;

   b) you're 62 or older, and the creditor will favor you because of your age;

   c) it's used to determine the meaning of other factors important to creditworthiness. For example, a creditor could use your age to determine if your income might drop because you're about to retire;

   d) it's used in a valid scoring system that favors applicants age 62 and older. For example, your length of employment might be scored differently depending on your age.

10. Refuse to consider public assistance income the same way as other income.

11. Discount income because of your sex or marital status. For example, a creditor cannot count a man's salary at 100% and a woman's at 75%. A creditor may not assume a woman of childbearing age will stop working to raise children.

12. Discount or refuse to consider income because it comes from part-time employment or pension, annuity, or retirement benefits programs.

13. Refuse to consider regular alimony, child support, or separate maintenance payments. A creditor may ask you to prove you have received this income consistently.

You Also Have The Right To:

1. Have credit in your birth name (Mary Smith), your first and your spouse's last name (Mary Jones), or your first name and a combined last name (Mary Smith-Jones).

2. Get credit without a co-signer, if you meet the creditor's standards.

3. Have a co-signer other than your husband or wife, if one is necessary.

4. Keep your own accounts after you change your name, marital sta-

tus, reach a certain age, or retire, unless the creditor has evidence that you're not willing or able to pay.

5. Know whether your application was accepted or rejected within 30 days.

6. Know why your application was rejected within 60 days.

7. Find out why you were offered less favorable terms than you applied for.

8. Find out why your account was closed or why the terms of the account were made less favorable.

If You Suspect Discrimination:

• Complain to the creditor. Make it known you're aware of the law. The creditor may find an error or reverse the decision.

• Check with your state Attorney General to see if the creditor violated state equal credit opportunity laws. Your state may decide to prosecute the creditor.

• Bring a case in federal district court. If you win, you can recover damages, including punitive damages.

• Join with others and file a class action suit. You may recover punitive damages for the group of up to $500,000 or one percent of the creditor's net worth, whichever is less.

The Fair Credit Billing Act (FCBA) - 15 U.S.C. § 1637 [3]

The Fair Credit Billing Act provides for prompt correction of billing mistakes, the withholding of payments for defective goods, and requires creditors to credit payments promptly. It also sets forth your rights and responsibilities when you lose your credit card or are the victim of credit card fraud. Most importantly, it protects your credit rating during the settling of the dispute.

The law applies to "open end" credit accounts, such as credit cards, and revolving charge accounts. It *does not* cover installment contracts — loans or extensions of credit you repay on a fixed schedule.

Types of errors covered under this law are:

1. Unauthorized charges. Federal law limits your responsibility for unauthorized charges to $50;

2. Charges that list the wrong date or amount;

3. Charges for goods and services you didn't accept or weren't delivered as agreed;

4. Math errors;

5. Failure to post payments and other credits, such as returns;

6. Failure to send bills to your current address, provided the creditor receives your change of address, in writing, at least 20 days before the billing period ends.

7. Charges for which you ask for an explanation or written proof of purchase along with a claimed error or request for clarification.

Other Billing Rights - Businesses that offer "open end" credit also must:

1. Give you a written notice when you open a new account.

2. Provide a statement for each billing period in which you owe, or they owe you more than one dollar;

3. Send your bill at least 14 days before the payment is due if you have a period within which to pay the bill without incurring additional charges;

4. Credit all payments to your account on the date they're received, unless no extra charges would result if they failed to do so.

5. Promptly credit or refund overpayments and other amounts owed to your account. This applies to instances where your account is owed more than one dollar. If you prefer a refund, it must be sent within seven business days after the creditor receives your written request. The creditor must also make a good faith effort to refund a credit balance that has remained on your account for more than 6 months.

What happens while the bill is in dispute?

You may withhold payment on the disputed amount (and related charges), during the investigation. However, you must pay any part of the bill not in question, including finance charges on the undisputed amount.

An important caveat:

Disputes about the quality of goods and services are not "billing errors," so the dispute procedure does not apply. However, if you buy unsatisfactory goods or services with a credit or charge card, you can take the same legal actions against the card issuer as you can take under state law against the seller.

What to do if you believe your rights have been violated under this Act

*   Write to the creditor at the address given for "billing inquiries," *not* the address for sending your payments, and include your name, address, account number and a description of the billing error.

*   Send your letter by certified mail, return receipt requested, so that it reaches the creditor within 60 days after the first bill containing the error was mailed to you. Include copies (not originals) of sales slips or other documents that support your position. Keep a copy of your dispute letter.

*   The creditor must acknowledge your complaint in writing within 30 days after receiving it, unless the problem has been resolved. The creditor must resolve the dispute within two billing cycles (but not more than 90 days) after receiving your letter.

*   You can sue a creditor who violates the FCBA. If you win, you may be awarded damages, plus twice the amount of any finance charge—as long as it's between $100 and $1,000. The court also may order the creditor to pay your attorney's fees and costs.

The Fair Debt Collection Practices Act (FDCPA) – 15 U.S.C. § 1692 – 1692o [4]

The Fair Debt Collection Practices Act ensures that debt collectors treat consumers fairly. This Act provides the greatest amount of protection, but it is frequently abused, and is very difficult to challenge.

What debts are covered? Personal, family, and household debts are covered under the Act. This includes money owed for the purchase of an automobile, for medical care, or for charge accounts.

Who is a debt collector? A debt collector is any person who regularly collects debts owed to others. This includes attorneys who collect debts on a regular basis.

How may a debt collector contact you? A collector may contact you in person, by mail, telephone, telegram, or fax. However, a debt collector may not contact you at inconvenient times or places, such as before 8 a.m. or after 9 p.m., unless you agree. A debt collector also may not contact you at work if the collector knows that your employer disapproves of such contacts.

Can you stop a debt collector from contacting you? You can stop a debt collector from contacting you by writing a letter to the collector telling them to stop. Once the collector receives your letter, they may not contact you again except to say there will be no further contact or to notify you that the debt collector or the creditor intends to take some specific action. Please note, however, that sending such a letter to a collector does not make the debt go away if you actually owe it. You could still be sued by the debt collector or your original creditor.

May a debt collector contact anyone else about your debt? If you have an attorney, the debt collector must contact the attorney, rather than you. If you do not have an attorney, a collector may contact other people, but only to find out where you live, what your phone number is, and where you work. Collectors usually are prohibited from contacting such third parties more than once. In most cases, the collector may NOT tell anyone other than you and your attorney that you owe money.

What must the debt collector tell you about the debt? Within 5 days after you are first contacted, the collector must send you a written notice telling you the amount of money you owe; the name of the creditor to whom you owe the money; and what action to take if you believe you do not owe the money.

May a debt collector continue to contact you if you believe you do not owe money? A collector may not contact you if, within 30 days after you receive the written notice, you send the collection agency a letter stating you do not owe money. However, a collector can renew collection activities if you are sent proof of the debt.

What types of debt collection practices are prohibited?

1. **Harassment**. Debt collectors may not:

    a) use threats of violence or harm;

    b) publish a list of consumers who refuse to pay their debts; or

    c) use obscene or profane language; or repeatedly use the telephone to annoy someone.

2. **False Statements**. Debt collectors may not:

    a) falsely imply that they are attorneys or government representatives;

    b) falsely imply that you have committed a crime;

    c) falsely represent that they operate or work for a credit bureau;

    d) misrepresent the amount of your debt;

    e) indicate that papers being sent to you are legal forms when they are not;

    f) indicate that papers being sent to you are not legal forms when they are;

    g) falsely imply that you will be arrested if you do not pay your debt;

    h) falsely imply that they will seize, garnish, attach, or sell your property or wages, unless the collection agency or creditor intends to do so, and it is legal to do so;

    i) falsely imply actions, such as a lawsuit, will be taken against you, when such action legally may not be taken, or when they do not intend to take such action;

    j) give false credit information about you to anyone, including a credit bureau;

    k) send you anything that looks like an official document

from a court or government agency when it is not; or

l) use a false name.

3. **Unfair practices.** Debt collectors may not:

a) collect any amount greater than your debt, unless your state law permits such a charge;

b) deposit a post-dated check prematurely;

c) use deception to make you accept collect calls or pay for telegrams;

d) take or threaten to take your property unless this can be done legally; or

e) contact you by postcard.

What to do if you believe your rights have been violated under this Act

You have the right to sue a collector in a state or federal court within one year from the date the law was violated. If you win, you may recover money for the damages you suffered plus an additional amount up to $1,000. Court costs and attorney's fees can also be recovered. A group of people may form a class action and sue a debt collector to and recover damages up to $500,000, or one percent of the collector's net worth, whichever is less.

The Credit Repair Organizations Act (CROA) -15 U.S.C. § 1679-1679j [5]

The Credit Repair Organizations Act was signed into law in 1996 to protect the consumers from unfair or deceptive advertising and business practices by credit repair organizations. By law, credit repair organizations:

• Cannot make false or misleading claims about their services.

• Cannot charge you fees for credit repair work that has not been provided.

• Must give you a 3-day cooling off period for you to change your mind after you have signed up.

Their contracts must clearly define:

1. The payment terms for credit repair.

2. The credit repair services to be performed.

3. How long it will take to achieve the results.

4. Guarantees offered.

5. The company name and contact information.

The Health Insurance Portability And Accountability Act Of 1996 (HIPAA) – Public Law 104-191 [6]

In August 1996, President Clinton signed into law the Health Insurance Portability and Accountability Act (HIPAA). The Act creates national standards to protect individuals' medical records and other personal health information.

1. It gives patients more control over their health information.

2. It sets boundaries on the use and release of health records.

3. It establishes appropriate safeguards that health care providers and others must achieve to protect the privacy of health information.

4. It holds violators accountable with civil and criminal penalties that can be imposed if they violate patients' privacy rights.

5. And it strikes a balance when public responsibility supports disclosure of some forms of data for example, to protect public health.

Where this relates to credit is when a medical facility violates your privacy by sending information to a collection agency that you did not authorize.

What to do if you believe your rights have been violated under this Act

File a complaint to the Office for Civil Rights (OCR). Your complaint must:

• Be filed in writing, either on paper or electronically;

• Must name the entity that is the subject of the complaint and describe the acts or omissions believed to be in violation of the applicable requirements of the Privacy Rule; and

- Be filed within 180 days of when you knew that the act or omission complained of occurred. OCR may extend the 180-day period if you can show "good cause."

The Office for Civil Rights has several regional offices, and each regional office covers certain states. You should send your complaint to the appropriate OCR Regional Office, based on the region where the alleged violation took place. Visit their HIPAA website at http://www.hhs.gov/ocr/hipaa for contact numbers and addresses.

THE REAL DEAL

The credit bureaus and creditors are in business because of us and for us. It's our records that make them money and they are obligated to report our records correctly and fix errors in a timely fashion. When you raise an issue with the credit bureaus or a creditor and they refuse to back down, even though you know you are right, you have an obligation to yourself to exercise your right to protect your name and your credit worthiness.

Taking on a big corporation can be very intimidating, but if you can prove your case then their size actually works against them. If the law is on your side, they will stand to lose a lot, and they know it. The best part is that now you know it, too!

[1]http://www.ftc.gov/os/statutes/fcrajump.shtm
[2]http://www.ftc.gov/bcp/edu/pubs/consumer/credit/cre15.shtm
[3]http://www.ftc.gov/bcp/edu/pubs/consumer/credit/cre16.shtm
[4]http://www.ftc.gov/bcp/edu/pubs/consumer/credit/cre18.shtm
[5]http://www.ftc.gov/os/statutes/croa/croa.shtm
[6]http://www.hhs.gov/ocr/privacysummary.pdf

CHAPTER 14

Statute Of Limitations & The 7-Year Reporting Period

How long will that collection remain on my report?

How long will that bankruptcy hurt my scores?

How long will I have to wait before my credits scores recover from that derogatory?

How long before I can see a clean credit report?

How long? How long? How long?

Everyone wants to know how long negative items can REALLY be reported. By the time you are finished with this chapter, you will have a very good understanding of one of the most misunderstood aspects of the Fair Credit Reporting Act: Statute of Limitations and The 7-Year Reporting Period.

Understanding the two can be the most powerful weapon you have to fight your case when it comes to improving your credit scores.

What's The Difference?

Many consumers confuse the 7-Year Reporting Period (also known as the Running of Reporting Period) with the Statute of Limitations on time allowed to legally collect a debt. The two are very different and should be understood clearly before entering into a credit improvement plan. Here's the difference:

1. The Statute of Limitations is the time period in which a creditor or collection agency has to use legal recourse—such as filing a lawsuit or judgment—against a consumer to collect a debt.

2. The 7-Year Reporting Period is the time allowed for derogatory items to remain on your credit reports.

Statute Of Limitations – Time Allowed To Legally Collect A Debt

Most derogatory debt expires. This doesn't mean that the creditor or collection agency cannot continue to try and collect the debt, or must remove it from your credit report. It means that they cannot file a lawsuit against you any longer, or garnish your wages or bank accounts. And, if the debt has expired, they cannot report it to the credit bureaus if they did not do so prior to expiration.

Different types of debts have different statute of limitations, so it is important to understand what the different categories are when you are trying to figure out what the statute is. And although there are several categories, for the purpose of this chapter I will refer only to the types of debt that are covered at length in this book.

- **Open-Ended Accounts** – These are revolving lines of credit with varying balances. The best example is a credit card account. Under the Truth-in-Lending Act, credit card accounts are always considered open-ended.

- **Written Contracts** – You agree to pay on a loan under the terms written in a document, which you and your debtor have signed. Examples are auto loans and other types of installment loans.

- **Promissory Notes** – You agree to pay on a loan through a written contract. However, the difference between a promissory note and a regular written contract is that the scheduled payments and interest on the loan are completely spelled out in the promissory note. A mortgage is an example of a promissory note.

- **Judgments** – If you have a judgment against you on your credit report, it means that a creditor or collection agency has taken you to court, sued you, and won the case against you. Some states allow creditors to renew judgments a second time, or even for an indefinite period of time. This means that a creditor can hold you accountable for a debt for a significant period of time, and even for the rest of your life! However, as you will read below, paid judgments must be removed from your credit report 7 years from the date satisfied.

To complicate it even further, each state may have a different statute of limitations on each type of debt. In some states, it's 3 years for an open-ended contract (i.e., credit cards), and 6 years for a written contract. Please realize that aside from the times allowed, each state also may have different laws regarding jurisdiction. For example, if you move out of state, the statute may stop temporarily, and if you ever move back that statute may pickup where it left off. Or, if the agreement was made in a different state, the laws of your current state may still apply. It's best to check your state statute requirements, as well as those for any states you might be considering for future residence. It's important to make sure that you check all of these items before expending energy or finances on pursuing legal action against a creditor, credit bureau or collection agency.

When Does The Statute Of Limitations Start?

In most instances, the statute of limitations start date is triggered by the date of last delinquency, however, state laws vary, so it is important to do your research.

Examples:

1. On a credit card account, it is the first 30-day late that leads to a charge-off or collection.

2. If it is a one-time billing, such as a medical bill, or a monthly billing, such as a utility bill, it is on the date that the bill first became past due which is usually 30 days from the original statement date. If the company doesn't send it to collections for two years, the statute still starts on the first past due date.

3. If it is a collection that has been sold from one company to another, the above rules still apply. They cannot renew the date of last delinquency by selling it.

4. Individual accounts that have been included in a bankruptcy fall under the same rules as all other accounts.

Renewing The Statute Of Limitations

In a book filled with dozens of very important lessons, this is perhaps the single most important one.

Be very careful about what you say and do when it comes to a delinquent account or a collection. Once the statute starts on an account, if you make a partial payment on it, or make a written or verbal promise to pay it, chances are you will reset the statute of limitations back to day one. That means that the creditor will be able to file a lawsuit against you, or garnish your wages, and trust me, they will.

This is a terrible mistake that consumers make every day because they just want to get collectors off of their backs. It is common practice for collection agencies to trick people into making a small *good-faith* payment. They do so because they know that once the agreement or payment is made, they can legally begin pursuing that person for collection. So, the best advice I can give you is to NEVER presume kindness from collectors. They are NOT your friends. They are only nice when they think they can get you to drop your guard and agree to something that will ultimately lead to: 1) a commission check for them; and 2) full payment on a debt that is no longer legally collectable.

The following table lists in years the statute of limitations for each state that were in effect at the time of writing this book. Please remember, statutes can be amended, so be sure to check the current statutes with your State's Attorney General site prior to using it as a legal defense in court. You can find direct links on my website at http://www.lindaferrari.com.

The Statute Of Limitations Table By State (In Years)

State	Written	Promissory	Open-Ended	Judgments
Alabama	6	6	3	20
Alaska	6	6	6	5
Arizona	6	5	3	10
Arkansas	5	6	3	10
California	4	4	4	10
Colorado	6	6	6	20
Connecticut	6	6	6	20
Delaware	3	6	3	-
DC	3	3	3	3
Florida	5	5	4	20

Georgia	6	6	4	7
Hawaii	6	6	6	10
Idaho	5	10	4	6
Illinois	10	6	5	20
Indiana	10	10	6	20
Iowa	10	5	5	20
Kansas	5	5	3	5
Kentucky	15	15	5	15
Louisiana	10	10	3	10
Maine	6	6	6	20
Maryland	3	6	3	12
Massachusetts	6	6	6	20
Michigan	6	6	6	10
Minnesota	6	6	6	10
Mississippi	3	3	3	7
Missouri	10	10	5	10
Montana	8	8	5	10
Nebraska	5	6	4	5
Nevada	6	3	4	6
New Hampshire	3	6	3	20
New Jersey	6	6	6	20
New Mexico	6	6	4	14
New York	6	6	6	20
North Carolina	3	5	3	10
North Dakota	6	6	6	10
Ohio	15	15	-	20
Oklahoma	5	5	3	5
Oregon	6	6	6	10
Pennsylvania	6	4	6	4
Rhode Island	15	10	10	20
South Carolina	10	3	3	10
South Dakota	6	6	6	20
Tennessee	6	6	6	10
Texas	4	4	4	10
Utah	6	6	4	8
Vermont	6	5	6	8

Virginia	5	6	3	20
Washington	6	6	3	10
West Virginia	10	6	5	10
Wisconsin	6	10	6	20
Wyoming	10	10	8	5

(Source: Direct Research of each state law.)

7-Year Reporting Period – Time Allowed To Remain On Your Credit Report

The second time period that you need to understand is the time allowed for derogatory items to remain on your credit report.

The time period legally allowed depends on the date of original delinquency of the account. The problem is, most people don't keep records and proving your case becomes very difficult, and when collections are sold over and over again, it becomes even more difficult to prove what that original date of delinquency was.

However, if you believe that the date of last activity that has been reported on a derogatory account is inaccurate, but you do not have proof, be sure to pay attention to the Validation of Debt Process (VOD) I describe in Chapter 18. In the instance of accounts sold to collection agencies, it gives you a way of getting access to the original account information.

When Does the 7-Year Reporting Period Start?

Here's the law:

> **Fair Credit Reporting Act Section 605. Requirements relating to information contained in consumer reports [15 U.S.C. §1681c]**
>
> (c) Running of Reporting Period
>
> (1) In general. *The 7-year period* referred to in paragraphs (4) and (6) 3 of subsection (a) *shall begin*, with respect to any delinquent account that is placed for collection (internally or by referral to a third-party, whichever is earlier), charged to profit and loss, or subjected to any similar action, *upon the expiration of the 180-day period beginning on the date of the commencement of the delinquency*

which immediately preceded the collection activity, charge to profit and loss, or similar action.

What this means is that the 7-year clock starts ticking 180 days from the date (month and year) of the first missed payment that led to charge off, collection, foreclosure or repossession. So, when you do the math, it is really 7 ½ years (from the last missed payment) that you can expect the derogatory item to come off of your credit report.

On a one-time billing type account (i.e. a medical bill, utility bill, etc.) the 7-year clock begins running 7 years from the date the account became past due, even if the creditor does not send the account to collection in a timely manner, this rule still applies.

In the case of late pays on accounts that do not result in a collection or charge-off, the 7-year clock begins running on the date that you were late.

Can The 7-Year Reporting Period Be Renewed?

In all of my research and years in this business, I have only seen one section of the U.S. Code that refers to having the 7-Year Reporting Period renewed. Title 20> Chapter 28> Subchapter IV, the code on Education. The following section refers to the amount of time a defaulted student loan can be reported on a credit report:

§ 1080a(f)(3) In the case of a borrower who reenters repayment after defaulting on a loan and subsequently goes into default on such loan, *7 years from the date the loan entered default such subsequent time.*

Other than the above exception, the 7-year clock cannot be renewed *under any circumstances*, even if the statute of limitations is accidentally renewed.

Regardless of how long a creditor waits to charge off, sell or transfer a debt, *they must report the true and correct "delinquent or last missed payment" date* (month and year) that preceded the creditor's action. If they do not, they can be held liable, and they know it.

Here's the law taken directly from the Fair Credit Reporting Act that addresses this issue:

605. Requirements relating to information contained in consumer reports [15 U.S.C. §1681c]

(a) Information excluded from consumer reports. Except as authorized under subsection (b) of this section, *no consumer reporting agency may make any consumer report containing any of the following items of information*:

(1) Cases under title 11 [United States Code] or under the Bankruptcy Act that, from the date of entry of the order for relief or the date of adjudication, as the case may be, antedate the report by more than 10 years.

(2) Civil suits, civil judgments, and records of arrest that from date of entry, *antedate the report by more than seven years or until the governing statute of limitations has expired*, whichever is the longer period.

(3) Paid tax liens which, from date of payment, antedate the report *by more than seven years*.

(4) Accounts placed for collection or charged to profit and loss which antedate the report *by more than seven years*.

(5) Any other adverse item of information, other than records of convictions of crimes which antedates the report *by more than seven years*.

Exceptions To The 7-Year Rule

1. Bankruptcies can remain on your record for up to 10 years from the date of discharge. Although, in my experience the three credit bureaus will remove a Chapter 13 Bankruptcy after 7 years.

2. Federal Tax Liens can remain for 7 years from the date paid; however, if not paid, they will remain for up to 10 years.

3. State Tax Liens are different from Federal Tax Liens. State tax liens can remain for 7 years from the date paid. However, if they are unpaid, they can remain indefinitely. Additionally, state tax liens may be governed by state law.

4. Information about a lawsuit or an unpaid judgment against you can be reported for 7 years from the date paid or until the statute of limitations runs out, whichever is longer. Remember, unpaid judgments can be renewed.

THE REAL DEAL

How long before I can have my life the way I want it? It's an important question to ask.

You have probably heard the expression, "Time heals all wounds." Even in the impersonal world of credit, this saying holds true. The most important aspect about Statute of Limitations and the 7-Year Reporting Period when it comes to credit issues is to know that they are there and must be considered. Know how long you will have to face derogatory reports. Know how long you will have to deal with that bankruptcy on your record.

An awareness of these important dates can be an invaluable tool that will enable you to dispute and win. You will be able to arrange your life's plans around the statutes; you will know how worthwhile it is to negotiate a deletion; you will know when to tell the creditors that they no longer have the right to report a record; you will know *how long*.

CHAPTER 15

Overextended?
Debt Relief Options & How
They Affect Credit Scores

We've all seen the commercials. You know, the ones where commerce slows to a screeching halt because someone has the audacity to pay with cash. We have become an entire society of card swipers. And, let's be honest, there's nothing more convenient than just spotting what you want, swiping your card, and presto, it's all yours. A quick run into the local coffee house for your morning caffeine infusion, a dash to the grocery store, an item that you had no intention of buying, but you had the card and you really wanted it. You know the story.

Credit card companies have made it effortless for consumers to quickly and efficiently charge themselves into oblivion, and without a second thought.

Here's the problem. When you receive your new credit card in the mail, the card company highlights in the large font the many *advantages* to using their card, while hiding the pitfalls in the *get out the magnifying glass section* of the really boring looking stuff that looks like it should be tossed in the trash.

Most people are lured in by the hope that they will finally have a credit instrument that will give them a low rate, an understanding creditor, and a plan that will, once and for all, allow them to get ahead. They fall for the hype and become easy pickings for default interest rates, exorbitant late fees, and a potential universal default.

I have always been a strong proponent of credit card use for achieving and maintaining strong credit scores. However, it is mission critical that you always live within and preferably below your means. But, the lure of consumerism with ease has caused so many Americans to exceedingly spend more than they make, causing them to fall victim to long-term indebtedness.

The statistics on consumer debt paint a grim picture. Per The Federal reserve as of August, 2008, Americans held $968 billion dollars in consumer credit card debt.[1] This number does not include loans secured by real estate, such as a mortgage. Another alarming statistic is that in the first quarter of 2008, consumer borrowing was at $34 billion, the most since the first three months of 2001, when the economy entered its last official recession. (*Source: http://www.federalreserve.gov*)

These numbers indicate that consumers need a clear understanding of consumer debt and relief options. Obviously, most people charge their lives away with the very best of intentions. Most people want to do the right thing. They want to provide themselves and their families the things they need, and even a few of the things they really want. And when you work hard, and you have every reason to think that your paycheck will come though over time and allow you to pay for those things, you go ahead and charge them. Very few of us look into the future and foresee a job layoff, a debilitating illness or accident, or some other economic circumstance that will deprive us of our ability to keep up with our bills. But these circumstances do happen and it is critically important that you know how to handle your debts should an unfortunate circumstance strike your world.

Understanding The Pitfalls of Consumer Debt

The first order of business for you is to understand the obligations and pitfalls of indebtedness:

- **Minimum Monthly Payments.** The Federal Government approved credit card companies to increase the minimum monthly payment on credit card accounts from 2-4%. This was done in an attempt to lower the amount of consumer debt per household. How much breathing room does this leave you?

- **Credit's True Cost.** According to CNN's credit card debt calculator at http://cgi.money.cnn.com/tools/debtplanner/debtplanner.jsp, if you have a $10,000 credit card balance with an 18% interest rate, by making minimum payments only, it will take you 12 years and 3 months to pay off that balance. And in that time, you will pay a total of $5,463.25 in interest.

- **Universal Default.** We talked about this in more detail in Chapter 8, where credit card companies are allowed to increase the rate of interest you pay to the highest amount possible if your credit scores go down, or if you are late on another credit card account. This extremely punitive measure is the primary reason why consumers end up declaring bankruptcy, charging off or entering into a credit counseling program.

- **Spending Limits.** Credit card companies give you a limit. Naturally, you would presume that you can spend up to your limit without being penalized. This is not the case. As outlined in Chapter 7, if you use up your limit, or max out your card, your credit scores will drop and all of your interest rates on ALL of your other cards will go up.

- **Creditor Communication.** Most major creditors refuse to enter into any type of negotiation with consumers until they are in default status. This means that people have to incur several late pays and a charge off before creditors are willing to talk to them about a solution. This is crazy.

So, there are a few traps out there. What are you options if you fall into a trap that finds you stuck in consumer debt hell with no easy way out?

Can You Do It On Your Own?

There is no doubt that you can create, implement and manage your own debt relief plan. I am a true believer in trying to do it on your own if you have the time because no one will have your back like you will. All you have to do is lay your debts out on paper, figure out how much you can realistically afford to pay, call the creditors to discuss your options or negotiate, get the agreement in writing, and then follow through with the payment plan as agreed. It does not take a specific degree to get the job done. However, there is a clear precedent set years ago by the credit counseling industry that makes creditors very reluctant to deal directly with consumers. But a precedent is not a law, and if you do your research, and work hard enough, you can definitely do it on your own.

The key to a successful debt relief negotiation is to establish clear goals before you start, and be persistent. Many times you may have to contact the creditors or collection agencies several times before reaching an agreement. Be professional even when they are not. Do not let your emotions get the best of you. Be polite, calm, and cool.

I would suggest trying it with at least one creditor prior to making the decision to turn your financial well-being over to someone else. If you are successful, then great! You will know whether or not it is something you can, or want to do. On the other hand, if you don't have the time, or emotional energy to face creditors and collection agencies head-on, you do have options and my best advice in this case is that you do as much research and cost comparison as possible before hiring a company, and that you make sure to do the math on the plans they propose. In other words, make sure that at the end of the day, the payment plans, or fees make sense.

Here are some great resources to help you get to know the ins and outs of the industry:

- National Foundation for Credit Counseling: http://www.nfcc.org

- Association of Independent Consumer Credit Counseling Agencies: http://www.aiccca.org

- The Federal Trade Commission: http://www.ftc.gov/credit

- National Consumer Law Center: http://www.consumerlaw.org

- Consumer Federation of America's Report: Credit Counseling in Crisis http://www.consumerfed.org/pdfs/credit_counseling_report.pdf

- National Consumer Law Centers Report: The ABC's of Credit Counseling http://www.consumerlaw.org/issues/credit_counseling/content/creditcounsconsumerconcernsAUG8.pdf

Debt Relief Options – How They Affect Credit Scores & Linda's Opinion

Remember, this is first and foremost a book about credit. I do touch on subjects such as budgeting and financial options, but I am not an expert in these areas and I would recommend you seek professional advice through other books or experts for this information.

There are several types of debt relief programs offered by professional companies. It can be very confusing to readily understand the differences between the various options because they all seem quite similar to the casual observer. In this book, I address the top five debt relief options, including how they work and how they affect your credit:

1. Debt Consolidation

2. Credit Counseling (AKA: Debt Management Plan)

3. Debt Settlement

4. Bankruptcy

5. Debt Negotiation

Here's the low down on each of those five options.

Option 1 – Debt Consolidation

Debt Consolidation is taking out a loan to pay off other debt that is usually credit card debt. It is often done:

- To save money that would normally be paid for high interest rates on credit cards;

- To eliminate paying several bills each month vs. one;

- Because you cannot afford the high interest rates and will default soon if you don't lower your payments.

Consumer options for Debt Consolidation are as follows:

1. **Take out a personal loan**. If you have good credit, this option is easy and the new credit will only affect your credit scores by a few points for a couple of months as long as you make payments on time.

2. **Apply for a Home Equity Line of Credit**. If you are a homeowner, and you have good credit, applying for a HELOC is another way to consolidate debt.

3. **Apply for a credit card** with a very high limit and a low, or no interest rate offer. Again, if you have good credit, this is an option for you if the credit card offer is great. Remember, however, if the balance

on the new card will be over 50% of the available limit when you transfer all of your other accounts over, your scores will go down.

If the credit card accounts you are paying through debt consolidation have high balances, your credit scores will go up when you pay those balances off. Remember, as discussed in Chapter 7, *do not* close any credit card accounts, even if you are not going to use them anymore.

CREDIT TIP

As discussed in Chapter 10, it is not a good idea to add auto and other installment debt to a debt consolidation loan. Installment loans are an important addition to your mix of credit.

Linda's Opinion

Debt Consolidation is a good option for those who are financially stable, have good credit, and good credit management skills. However, it is not an option that will improve a bad financial situation because all you are doing is moving your debt around. Before you undertake a debt consolidation plan, be very clear about your objectives and whether they can be realistically met through debt consolidation.

I highly recommend that you first consider calling your credit card companies to try and work out a reduced interest rate plan. Some will offer you a temporary deferral of lower interest rates for 4-6 months. However, remember that the rates will go right back up when the deferral time has expired. A better option is to get them to lower your interest rates permanently. Be sure to advise them that you will be taking your business elsewhere. This provides you with a good chance of getting them to oblige, as they probably do not want to see the business walk away. I have seen it happen on several occasions.

However, if your sole purpose for consolidating your debt is because you are buried in high interest rates and are starting to fall behind, then I don't think that this is a good option for you, unless you know for certain that you will be in a stronger financial position within the next 4-6 months. Most likely, if you are over-extended financially, your credit card balances are maxed out; meaning your credit scores will be too low to qualify for one of the options above. In this case, I advise that you look into a Credit Counseling Program.

Option 2 - Credit Counseling

If any two or three of the following items apply to you, Credit Counseling may be a good option.

- You are living paycheck to paycheck and cannot get ahead.
- You are still current on accounts, but will become past due very soon.
- You are over the limit on your credit card accounts.
- You have no, or very few late payments.
- You have high interest rates that keep going up.
- You are starting to receive collection calls from creditors or collection notices from collection agencies.
- You do not have the time or skills to create a budget or money management plan that will work.
- You are not comfortable dealing directly with creditors to find a solution to your current financial situation.

Credit Counseling is a service provided by organizations to help consumers find ways to repay their debts through careful budgeting and management of money. Credit counseling is an industry that is under severe scrutiny and should be entered into with caution. The resources above will be a great starting place to do your research in finding a reputable and trustworthy agency to help.

Only unsecured lines of credit are eligible for credit counseling plans. This includes credit cards, personal loans, medical bills, collection accounts, unpaid utilities, auto loans that have gone to repossession, and payday loans.

How Does Credit Counseling Work?

1. First, you have to select a credit counseling company to work with. Per The Federal Trade Commission, reputable credit counseling organizations advise you on managing your money and debts, help you develop a budget, and usually offer free educational materials and workshops. Their counselors are certified and trained in the areas of consumer credit, money and debt management, and budgeting. Counselors discuss your entire financial situation with you, and help you develop a

personalized plan to solve your money problems. An initial counseling session typically lasts an hour, with an offer of follow-up sessions.

A reputable credit counseling agency should send you free information about the services it provides without requiring you to provide any details about your situation. If a firm doesn't do that, consider it a red flag and go elsewhere for help.

Be sure to check out your prospective credit counselor with your state Attorney General, local consumer protection agency, and Better Business Bureau. They can tell you if consumers have filed complaints about them. (But even if there are no complaints about them, it's not a guarantee that they're legitimate.) The United States Trustee Program also keeps a list of credit counseling agencies that have been approved to provide pre-bankruptcy counseling.

2. Once you have selected a credit counseling company that you trust, you will then work with the credit counselor to create a workable payment plan with all of your existing unsecured debt that fits within your budget. The overall budget and analysis process will also take into consideration your income and expenses.

    When the plan is on paper, the credit counselor will work with you to negotiate reduced interest rates and payments with your creditors. They may even be able to remove late fees and penalties if you are already in default.

3. Once the new payment schedule is in place with the original creditors, you, the consumer, are responsible for making the agreed-to monthly payments to each creditor on time every month.

WORD OF CAUTION

If you default on the payment schedule that was implemented by a credit counseling company, you stand to lose all negotiated reductions and your interest rates, payments and fees will all reset to where they were when you first started.

4. If your debt is overwhelming or burdensome, the credit counseling agency may speak to you about entering into a Debt Manage-

ment Plan (DMP) with them. Instead of paying the creditors directly as outlined above, this plan would allow you to make a lump sum monthly payment to the credit counseling agency, and they would pay your creditors according to the agreed-upon payment schedule.

WORD OF CAUTION

Credit counseling agencies make a lot more money when consumers sign up for their DMPs, so it is common for credit counselors to mislead consumers into thinking that a DMP is their only option. You are not obligated to hire the credit counseling company to proceed with the debt management plan, especially if you believe that you are disciplined enough to stick to the payment schedule that was created during your credit counseling program. STICK TO YOUR GUNS. However, if you are very busy, or simply not good at paying your bills on time, it is recommended that you consider a DMP.

How Does Credit Counseling Affect Your Credit?

Per Fair Isaac & Co., the credit scoring software does not consider whether or not consumers are participating in a credit counseling program of any kind (see Chapter 6.) It's also important to remember that credit counseling agencies are not creditors and they do not report to the credit bureaus. So it is a myth that by contacting a credit counseling agency, your scores will go down.

So it all depends mainly on your credit at the time you enter into credit counseling. If you're past due on your bills, once you start making payments under the newly negotiated payment schedule, they will become current, and your scores will start to improve. But if you are current, and have not incurred any late pays, then credit counseling and debt management plans will not affect your credit scores, provided that you remain current.

One item to note is that once you enter into a negotiated payment schedule, all of your accounts will be closed. As we discussed in Chapter 7, open credit card accounts make up for almost 30% of your credit score, so unless you have accounts that are not under credit counseling that are still open, you will lose points for not having any open accounts.

WORD OF CAUTION

Be aware that if you enter into a debt management program with a credit counseling service, and you hire them to pay your creditors in a workout plan, if they pay that creditor late the creditors will report a late pay and your scores can drop instantly by as much as 80 points. There is nothing you can do about it short of suing the credit counseling company. This is why I want you to be certain that you conduct a thorough background search, work with the most reputable firm you can find, and be very deliberate and cautious before you turn your financial well being over to anyone.

When it comes to how Credit Counseling and DMP's are reflected in your credit reports, you can expect that debt management plans will show up as "Account handled by CCCS" or "Account on DMP," as a note or comment added by the creditor. This note intends to discourage lenders from enabling the individual to add additional lines of unsecured credit. However, this note will not affect your credit scores. Once the plan is completed, the note will be removed. If you enter into such a plan, make sure that you request copies of your reports once you have paid balances in full in order to make sure the note has been removed.

Pros Of Credit Counseling

1. You will have a repayment plan that you can live with, that will give you instant relief from your burdensome debt; one that would be very time consuming and difficult for you to negotiate on your own because creditors very rarely work with consumers directly to renegotiate interest rates and payments when consumers are in trouble.

2. You will be free of the stress of not being able to make your payments. You will be able to focus on the important things in life such as your family and your work without worrying about paying that stack of bills.

3. If you have not fallen behind on your accounts before entering into credit counseling, then your scores will only be affected very little due to the closing of your accounts. However, if you are in default, creditors will stop reporting you as paying late, once you start mak-

ing payment on the newly agreed to schedule. This way your negative history can start aging out.

CREDIT TIP

IMPORTANT: Before you enter into any agreement with a credit counseling firm: 1) make sure that you call your creditors to confirm the acceptability of the agreements the counseling firm has proposed, and 2) make sure that the creditors will, in fact, stop all negative reporting when you begin the new payment schedule.

---

4. Because of your efforts, you will stay in the good graces of your creditors and they will most likely be willing to do business with you again.

Cons Of Credit Counseling

1. A successful Credit Counseling or Debt Management Plan could take 48-60 months to complete. Many people have trouble knowing where they will be in the next month, let alone, the next 4-5 years. This is why the drop-out rate is very high. To be successful, these plans require a significant degree of budgeting and willpower.

2. There are more scam artists out there then there are reputable companies. They give the impression that they are saving you money by getting your monthly payments lowered, when, in most cases, the debt has just being stretched over a longer period of time. Let's say your current payment is $500.00 and the total could be paid over a period of 24 months. With credit counseling your payment may drop to say $250.00–but for 48-60 months. You could end up paying more.

3. When entering into a Credit Counseling or Debt Management Plan, in many instances you have to agree not to apply for any credit. That means that for 2-5 years, you cannot apply for a home loan, or re-establish your credit by applying for new credit to rebuild. However, everything is open to negotiation and should be discussed and agreed to up-front.

CREDIT TIP

Because all accounts included in credit counseling will be closed, I recommend that you do everything you can to keep at least one major credit card out of the plan so that you will continue to build your credit in the amounts owed factor as laid out in Chapter 7.

4. If you decide to enter into a Credit Counseling or Debt Management Plan and you decide at any point prior to the agreed end date to terminate the payment plan, unfortunately, because of the standards in the industry, most creditors will not continue to honor the agreements that they had made with the counseling agency. All of your interest rates and payments will be reset to the original amounts immediately. And remember, by this point, all of your accounts had been closed and most of your credit card interest rates will be reset back to the highest amount allowed. It becomes a bigger mess than the mess that drove you to the payment plan in the first place.

5. Credit Counseling Agencies are really working for the creditors and the banking industry from whom they make almost all of their profits. In addition to the fees that they charge consumers, their primary source of income comes from creditors. They receive a fee every time you make a payment. This is why once you stop making that payment, the creditors reset your account back to where it started. This double dealing forces consumers to question: If credit counselors receive fees based on how much consumers pay, what is their motivation to help consumers reduce their debt?

Linda's Opinion

Credit counseling can be a great option for those who suffer financial setbacks, and I strongly support this option if you can find an ethical company to work with and you start early enough. If you do so, you can save your credit.

Mainly, however, my thoughts regarding credit counseling are that it is a good option for someone who is facing a temporary financial set back. No more than 12-24 months.

Option 3 – Debt Settlement

Unlike credit counseling, which involves an immediate plan to pay the total amount due over time and with reduced interest rates, Debt Settlement companies will negotiate with the creditors to reach a reduced payoff balance once you have saved enough money to negotiate down your debts. An efficient debt settlement company can reduce the payable amount to 40-60% of your original amount, and *so can you!*

You are a candidate for Debt Settlement if:

* You are already delinquent on accounts by a few months.

* You have accounts that have already been charged-off or sent to collections.

* You are being threatened by lawsuit or judgment.

* You do not have the funds to pay the delinquent items in full.

In my vast experience, I believe that this option is not an option at all. It is a combination of Credit Counseling, which you can sometimes get for free, and Debt Negotiation, which you can do yourself. And if not, there are plenty of reputable companies out there that can help you negotiate debt.

How Does Debt Settlement Work?

1. To analyze your current situation, the debt settlement company will conduct the same process as that of a Credit Counseling company. They estimate how much they think they can reduce your debt through negotiation. From there, they consider that reduced rate in relation to your income and expenses so as to design an affordable monthly "savings plan" stretched over a period of 12-36 months.

2. If you decide to hire them, most debt settlement companies require that you make an agreement to deposit that amount into a trust account for the 12-36 month time period.

3. While you are in the program, you cannot make payments to your creditors. If you do, you stand to lose a good percentage of the monies you have deposited into the trust account.

4. Realizing that if you just stop paying your creditors they will start

calling and harassing you for money, most debt settlement companies offer to educate you on how to handle creditor calls and com-
munications. They will not speak to your creditors until you have
enough money in the trust account to pay the debt, and they are the
ones who make that decision, not you.

5. Once there is enough money in the account, the debt settlement
company will start negotiations with your creditors and will pay off
your debts one by one as the monies are available; usually 12-36
months, depending on which plan you are in.

How Does Debt Settlement Affect Your Credit?

To put it succinctly, debt settlement trashes your credit.

When you enter into a debt settlement program, the plan is to immediately stop paying your creditors. As such, you will continue to be reported
late, accounts will go to charge-off and collections, judgments could be filed
against you, and yes, you might be sued. Most likely, this is why debt settlement companies have you deposit your money into a trust account. This
way, the monies cannot be garnished or confiscated.

Pros Of Debt Settlement

None.

Cons Of Debt Settlement

Too many to list.

Linda's Opinion

I understand the thought behind this option, because I know how the system
works. If you stop paying your accounts they will go to charge-off and collection. Once they go to charge-off and collection, they are a snap to negotiate for professionals.

However, you are making a deal with the devil when you pay someone
to help you wreck your credit. If debt settlement is your only option (and I
don't think it ever is), then you can open up the bank account on your own,
devastate your credit, and save the money you would have paid the person

who profits by your devastation.

Option 4 – Bankruptcy

Plain and simple, bankruptcy is the most difficult option to choose; one you should avoid at all costs unless you are upside down on everything. This public record will wreak havoc on credit scores and can prevent people from being hired or being able to rent a place to live.

Sad but very true, bankruptcy has always been the most popular debt relief program. I am certain that this is the case because so many people either receive bad advice or just simply do not understand the other options available to them. When faced with this type of struggle, people become confused and frightened. They become so desperate to make the pain go away that they make bad choices, sometimes exacerbating the problem.

There are plenty of steps you can take to correct your situation before it results in bankruptcy. Bankruptcy should always be your last option.

I will talk more about how a bankruptcy affects credit scores in Chapter 16.

Option 5 – Debt Negotiation

Debt Negotiation occurs when you make an agreement with a creditor to pay less than the amount you owe—in one lump sum. In my professional experience, I have found that debts can be negotiated for between 20-60% of the original debt.

The current account status determines with whom you will negotiate and how you will negotiate. If the account has not been sent off to collection or charge-off yet, then you will negotiate with the original creditor. If the account is in collections or has been charged-off, then you will be negotiating with a collection agency or collection attorney.

You can always get a better deal once an account has been charged off or sent to collections, however, if there is any chance that you can save your credit by making an arrangement before it goes to collection, you should try that avenue.

You are a candidate for Debt Negotiation if:

• You are still current on accounts, but are just about to go into default for a long period of time due to financial hardship (loss of job, medical crisis, divorce).

It is true that most creditors make it very difficult to negotiate debts that are still open active accounts, but I have seen many clients successfully negotiate with their credit card companies to pay off accounts for less, and before they have actually defaulted on accounts. This is especially doable if they are upside down in their mortgage payments.

- You are already delinquent on accounts by a few months and do not foresee being able to catch up any time soon.

- You have accounts that have already been charged-off or sent to collections.

- You are being threatened by lawsuit or judgment.

How Does Debt Negotiation Work?

First, decide whether you will do the negotiating on your own or hire someone to do it for you. Debt negotiation is a strategic and a time-consuming process, and is easier to accomplish with limited emotional attachment involved. Collection agencies are ruthless, and will go to any extent to scare you into thinking that they will take away everything from you if you don't pay your debt in full today. If you find a reputable company, hiring a professional debt negotiator who is thoroughly trained to effectively and strategically work with creditors to reduce your debt is a benefit.

If you decide to work with a debt negotiation company, be sure to check it out with your state Attorney General, local consumer protection agency, and the Better Business Bureau. They can tell you if any consumer complaints are on file about the firm you're considering doing business with. Also, ask your state Attorney General if the company is required to be licensed to work in your state and, if so, whether it is.

Here is the process:

1. The debt negotiation company will work with you to create a list of the debts they will negotiate for you. Most debt negotiation companies will charge for their services at a rate of 15-18% of your total

debt. You will sign a contract that gives them power of attorney to negotiate on your behalf. This contract will set forth stipulations as to your actions during the process.

CREDIT TIP

THINK ABOUT IT: I have found that it is much better for you to work with a debt negotiator who charges a percentage of the amount they save you. By charging a percentage of total debt, they may lack the motivation to settle for less in a shorter period of time. In contrast, when a negotiator gets paid on how much they save you, they will work hard to save you more.

---

2. You will be required to deposit an established amount of money (usually 40-60% of the total debt) into a bank or escrow account to which they have access. Doing so ensures that the money is easily available when negotiation is complete.

3. Most often, the fee to get started is substantial. This is because debt negotiators will start working with all of your creditors immediately, and if you change your mind at the last minute they need to be paid for the time they spent negotiating on your behalf. For this reason, it is important that you conduct intense research on the person you intend to hire before you send them that fee.

4. When an agreement has been struck with one of your creditors, the debt negotiator should request a letter from the creditor confirming the agreement. Once this confirmation letter is received, funds will need to be available immediately via transfer, automatic withdraw, or overnight cashier's check.

5. The debt negotiator will receive a payoff letter and you will send that letter to the credit bureaus that are reporting the item asking that they update your credit report with the new information.

How Does Debt Negotiation Affect Your Credit?

Most likely, if you have entered into debt negotiations you are over-extended and even in default. How all of this affects your credit depends on the outcome of the negotiations, which can range as follows:

1. If you negotiate with original creditors on accounts still in good standing, they will *not* negotiate a deletion letter in exchange for payment. This is considered a "fresh" account, removal of which is not part of their policies or procedures. Successful negotiations with them may lead to a reduction in your total amount due by 40-60%, with one of the following credit reporting options:

    •   Paid For Less Than Total Amount Due

    •   Settlement Accepted On This Account

    •   Paid Settlement

    Each of the above ratings can instantly drop your credit scores by 100 points, depending on how many points you have to lose. If you have several accounts to negotiate, you will suffer a severe hit for the first account, but the drops for subsequent accounts settled will be less severe. Eventually, you will max out in your penalty for the Payment History Factor which is 297.5 points.

    The good news for your Payment History Factor is that once the negative reporting hits your credit reports, the 7-Year Reporting Period will commence, and the account will start aging out within 6 months. Also, if you handle your negotiations at this level, you will avoid additional negative activity spun off from the original account, such as collection or judgment.

CREDIT TIP

If you have a great relationship with your creditor, and you point out to them that by law they are not obligated to report negative information about you to the credit bureaus, you may be able to negotiate a Paid As Agreed reporting. (See Chapter 2 under Hardship.) If you succeed, and have not had any late pays on the account, your credit scores will only receive a small penalty for closing the account.

---

2. If you are negotiating with a collection agency, or collection attor-

ney, it means that the accounts have already been reported on your credit reports and your scores have already taken the initial hit of up to 100 points.

The good news about negotiation on a collection, especially one that is a couple of years old, is that you can negotiate payment in exchange for a deletion letter, which is the ultimate goal. If you are successful, your scores will go back up as soon as the credit bureaus delete the account from your credit file. (Read more in Chapter 18.)

Tips For Negotiating On Your Own

*   Never pay a collection or charge off that is more than a year old without first validating the account (more in Chapter 18.) The purpose of validation is to ensure:

    a) The debt belongs to you. You'd be surprised at how many times I have found collections on my clients' credit reports that do not belong to them. The collections come from identity theft issues, poor data entry, collection scams, you name it.

    b) The collection agency trying to collect the debt actually has legal right to do so.

    c) The amount they attempt to collect is fair, true, and accurate.

    d) The date they claim as last activity is accurate.

    As a matter of course, debt negotiation companies will not validate debts. So if you decide to work with a company you will have to validate your debts first.

*   In Chapter 14, we discuss statute of limitations. The older a delinquent account, the easier it is to negotiate the debt for a much lower amount. It is extremely important to know the accurate dates for when debts expire, and to use the validation of debt process outlined in Chapter 18 to find out what those dates are. If the statute of limitations has expired on a debt, you can achieve a significantly lower settlement. Why? Because once the statute has expired, the

creditor can no longer use legal tactics to collect. They would be lucky to recoup any amount on the debt at that point.

- Believe it or not, creditors are human. If your enrollment in a debt negotiation program is the direct result of circumstances that you could not control (divorce, medical issues, job loss) and you can document it, then you're far more likely to get a favorable settlement versus a person who the creditor feels could have paid the debt back in full. If a consumer has just been diagnosed with brain cancer the settlement in most cases will be quick and a lot more favorable. If you have an honest hardship, use it. And do it in writing.

- Never threaten bankruptcy with the original creditor. Doing so will do far more harm than good. However, when the debt goes to collections, it's perfectly fine to advise that a bankruptcy is an option for you if an extremely reasonable settlement cannot be reached.

- Use the knowledge that you have gained from this book.

  a) If the statute has expired, tell the collection agency that you know they can no longer legally pursue collection of that debt, or re-report it. It would be against the law.

  b) If the statute of limitations is in question, tell the collection agency that you are aware of your rights, and that if they can't prove their case you are not legally obligated to pay. Also inform them that they are legally restricted from reporting the account to the credit bureaus while the item is in question.

  c) Let them know you are very aware that if you pay an account that is over a year old your credit scores will drop, so unless they delete the account in exchange for payment you have no motivation to pay it, especially before putting them through the validation of debt process outlined in Chapter 18.

  d) If they tell you that, by law, they cannot delete an account, make sure you point out there is no language in the law that states a creditor must report negative information to the credit bureaus.

You are well armed to challenge creditors and collection agents when you know your rights.

Pros Of Debt Negotiation

- You pay less–in some cases far less– than what you owe.

- Paying off the negotiated debt immediately puts you in a position to leverage a letter for full deletion so the negative record can be completely stricken from your credit reports. This is much more difficult with payment plan options.

- You get rid of the debt immediately.

- You can start rebuilding your credit immediately.

- You can seek removal immediately.

Cons Of Debt Negotiation

- It's difficult, draining and exhausting.

- It's a very negative hit to your credit.

Linda's Opinion

Debt negotiation can be a very valuable tool. In fact, I think it's one of the best options available if you can pay off the negotiated debt and get a deletion letter at the same time. However, you will have to pay a lump sum, so if you don't have access to cash, you cannot enter into this type of agreement. This is why it is so critical to know all of your options prior to making any phone calls or contacting creditors or collection agents.

1099-C: Cancellation Of Debt Form – Internal Revenue Service Code

When it comes to negotiating debt, most consumers don't realize that when a creditor charges off all or part of a debt, it can report the unpaid amount as a tax loss to the IRS using a 1099-C: Cancellation of Debt Form. The IRS can treat a cancellation of a debt as income you have received even though you have not actually received the money.

Here are some frequently asked questions and tips that will give you some important answers to questions about Form 1099-C: [1]

Why would you receive a 1099-C: Cancellation of Debt Form?

If you have defaulted (failed to make payments as agreed) on a debt in the past and you have either reached a compromise with a creditor to settle your debt, or the creditor has deemed the debt to be non-collectable and has stopped attempts to recover, you may receive a 1099-C form. The IRS definition of a compromise in a collection case is the discharge of indebtedness under an agreement between the creditor and the debtor to cancel the debt at less than full consideration.

What is a 1099-C: Cancellation of Debt Form?

A 1099-C form lets you know that a creditor is going to write-off the remaining unpaid portion of your debt. A 1099-C: Cancellation of Debt Form is filed by a creditor with the IRS when a settlement agreement between a debtor and a creditor has been reached or when a creditor has determined that a debt will never be paid. If the debt is for $600 or more the creditor must send you, the debtor, a 1099-C in the mail by January 31st and to the IRS by February 28th of the tax year in which the debt was discharged.

What should you do after receiving a 1099-C: Cancellation of Debt Form?

If you receive a 1099-C form from a creditor, you must report the amount of the canceled debt as income to the IRS even though you have not actually received the money. (The amount shown in Box 2 of the 1099-C form is the amount that must be reported as income.)

What debts are forgiven under a 1099-C: Cancellation of Debt Form?

The IRS recognizes five situations where a cancelled debt does *not have to be reported* as income.

1. Bankruptcy – the debt was already discharged through a bankruptcy proceeding.

2. Insolvency – your total debts exceeded your total assets at the time

your debt was settled or deemed non-collectable.

3. Indebtedness is due to a qualified farm expense.

4. Indebtedness is due to certain real property business losses.

5. Discharge of your debt was treated as a gift.

How do you know if you are insolvent?

You are deemed to be insolvent if your total liabilities (debts) are greater than your total assets. For example, if your total liabilities are $8,000 and your total assets at the time are $6,000 you are insolvent in the amount of $2,000. To determine the value of your assets use the fair market value rather than what you paid for them or what you think they are worth.

If you are insolvent you need to explain this to the IRS in one of two ways: 1) By filling out IRS Form 982: Reduction of Tax Attributes Due to Discharge of Indebtedness; or 2) Attaching a detailed letter to your tax return explaining the calculation of your total debts and assets.

Helpful tips to avoid problems if you have received a 1099-C: Cancellation of Debt Form

- If you settle your debt for less than full consideration (paid in full) be sure to ask the creditor if they intend to submit a 1099-C Form to the IRS.

- Consider, if a debt compromise is in your best interest, or is it a smarter decision to pay the debt in full? Failure to report added income could end up costing you in the end.

- The name of the creditor may not be readily recognizable on the 1099-C Form. The creditor may have sold the debt to a third party collection agency or the name of the parent company could be listed as the creditor.

- Look to see if the added income received from a debt cancellation will move you into a higher tax bracket.

- You cannot claim that you never received a 1099-C Form in the mail. Even if you do not receive the 1099-C form you are expected to recognize a capital gain. This is why it is important to confirm with the creditor what their intentions are when it comes to filing a 1099-C Form.

- For individuals who receive public benefits and public housing—be sure to check if your updated income will exclude you from the benefits you are receiving.

Here's what you need to know:

- In my experience, very few creditors file a 1099-C Form for the following reasons:

    a) Per the IRS Code, a creditor should only file a 1099-C after they have stopped collection activity. Meaning that once a creditor files a 1099-C, they can no longer collect on the debt—AT ALL. Most creditors are not willing to give up collection efforts so quickly.

    b) Per the IRS Code, a creditor should only file a 1099-C when there has been no payment activity on the account for three years. Creditors are obligated to support their claim with full documentation—a process that can be very burdensome for creditors, because in most instances, they had written the debt off years earlier and the relevant records are or no longer readily accessible.

    c) I am not a tax specialist, however, logic would lead me to believe that a creditor would also be restricted from selling the debt to a collection agency after filing a 1099-C, because then it would make the amount listed as a loss on the form a *false amount*. In other words, if a creditor claims a $1000 loss, and they sell that debt to a collection company for $250, then the real loss becomes $750, not $1000. The paperwork involved in going back to amend a 1099-C that was filed years before would outweigh any benefit.

    Due to the recent mortgage crisis, new bankruptcy laws, and falling economy, I expect that more creditors will be filing 1099-C forms over the next few years. This makes it important for consumers to pay more attention to this issue when dealing with charged off debts.

- If a creditor files a 1099-C, they are required to provide a copy of the form to the debtor. However, if they don't send you a copy and the creditor has provided the information to the IRS, you may be audited, or receive a tax bill. This could end up costing you more (in IRS interest and penalties) in the long run. Claiming that you did not receive the copy in the mail is not an acceptable argument with the IRS. This is why it is important to confirm with the creditor what their intentions are when it comes to filing a 1099-C Form.

- If it is a collection agency that has filed a 1099-C, make sure that the amount they are claiming is true and accurate. Collection agencies pay pennies on the dollar for debts. Example: A collection agency will purchase a $1000 debt from the original creditor for $200. Then, the collection agency will in turn, try to collect $1000 plus fees and interest from you. However, if they never collect on the debt, then the true amount of the loss to the collection agency is what they paid for the debt—$200, not $1000. Now, if you agree to pay the collection agency $150 as payment in full for the debt, then the true amount of loss would be $50.

Bottom line: Most collection agencies do not file 1099-C forms, but some agencies are notorious for using the form as a threat in collection efforts. When dealing with a collection agency vs. the original creditor, if you do receive a 1099-C form, make sure that you check the amount that they are claiming as a loss.

- Pay careful attention to the fact that if you can prove insolvency, then you will not be required to report the charged off amount as income. This is a huge break for debtors, and should not be overlooked. All you need to do is make a list of your assets and their fair market values, and then list your debts. If your total debt exceeds your total assets, then you are considered to be insolvent.

Note: If the IRS is suspicious that you may have omitted assets or undervalued others they do not have to accept your numbers. Having the amounts verified by a CPA or other professional would strengthen your case.

The best advice I can give you about this issue is to ask. If you accept a settlement offer, or negotiate with a creditor to pay less for a debt, ask the creditor if they intend to file a 1099-C Form. Remind them that by law, they MUST send a copy of that form to you, and that they MUST report the loss at its true and accurate amount.

In addition, if you are in a position of having to settle a debt for less with a creditor, you can negotiate with them to *NOT* send the remainder as a loss to the IRS. They are not legally obligated to do so.

The code that governs this important tax concern is U.S. Code TITLE 26 > Subtitle A > CHAPTER 1 > Subchapter B > PART III > § 108. Income From Discharge of Indebtedness. You can read the code at http://www4.law. cornell.edu/uscode/26/usc_sec_26_00000108----000-.html.

Real Life Success Story: David

Debt Negotiation can create real life miracles. In fact, just two months before I began writing this book I received a call from a client I'll call David. David was in a situation in which he found himself a heartbeat away from throwing his hands up and walking away from everything. He had a failing business that had been in the red for more than two years, a home for which he now owed more than its value, four credit card accounts that were maxed out to the tune of $210,000, and a collapsed emotional and physical threshold.

We sat down and took a look at his debt, to see what we could do to salvage his credit and his life. The first question I asked David is how much cash he could gather to help settle his debts. He estimated that he could raise about $100,000 to settle $210,000 in credit card debt, and bring his mortgage current.

David had always been on top of the game. He usually had a lot of money, and he was strong. Because I knew this, I worked with David teaching him how to debt negotiate. At first he was reluctant, because the accounts were still open and in good standing. "There is no way that these banks are going to accept this offer from me, especially when I am still current on the accounts," David argued. "I have no idea what to say, or what to ask for. I want you to handle this for me."

I explained to David that to have a third-party call on behalf of his open accounts that were in good standing would immediately create a defensive situation. If anyone other than David made that first call, the chances of reaching a settlement amount on his accounts before they charged off would be very slim. So we wrote his hardship letter and mailed it to the creditors, and I coached David through the do's and don'ts of negotiating on the telephone. Within one week, he had successfully negotiated three of the accounts for 40%. He told me that he was honest and professional. I had advised him to not threaten bankruptcy straight out, but to make it clear that he did not foresee being able to pull himself out of his financial situation. I also suggested that he offer to send them proof of his hardship. Proof that his company had been in the red and that he was not pulling enough income to cover his debts, and proof that his mortgage was in default. Once David finished negotiating with the first creditor successfully, the remaining creditors were much easier to face. He now knew it was possible to do something that he had believed could not be done. He saved many thousands of dollars in commission fees to a debt negotiation company and he immediately reduced his debt by more than $60,000.

The accounts were reported to the credit bureaus as "Paid For Less Than Full Balance," which is negative, but less negative than a Charge Off or Collection with a balance that is open to lawsuit. Plus when the balances went down to zero, his score went up in the Amounts Owed factor because his debt to limit ratio on those accounts was at $0.

THE REAL DEAL

If there is one action I want you to implement after reading this chapter it is to keep your credit card debts in check, and at all times! Don't let your credit card debt get out of your control. Don't be so quick to swipe that card. Yes, I advocate that you use your credit cards, because I am a credit score expert, and the rules set forth by Fair Isaac & Co. are very clear. Consumers must have credit cards to maximize their credit scores. However, it is important that you always live within, if not below, your means.

The moment you sense a problem with your credit card debt, consider your options. If you feel that you would benefit from professional help, seek assistance from a reputable credit counseling agency as early as possible. This is the best way to avoid long-lasting problems.

There are many opportunities to correct your problems before you reach the dead end of bankruptcy. If you need help, I strongly advise you to act quickly, decisively, and intelligently so as to avoid more painful avenues that avoidance will force.

[1]http://www.federalreserve.gov/releases/G19/Current
[2] http://www.lsnv.org/Debt_Cancellation_Vignette.doc

CHAPTER 16

Bankruptcy

In Chapter 15, I advised that when faced with a difficult debt situation, bankruptcy should not even merit consideration until all other remedies have been well vetted. Even though bankruptcy should be a course of last resort, many unwitting consumers fall victim to this path.

Data from the Administrative Office of the U.S. Courts tells us that nearly a quarter of a million Americans filed for bankruptcy in the first quarter of 2008. Logically, we can assume that there will be over one million bankruptcies filed for the year as a whole. This number is up significantly from 2007, which saw about 850,000, and dramatically up from 2006 which saw about 620,000. [1]

A disturbing trend regarding bankruptcy is that they are on the rise, despite the sweeping bankruptcy reform laws that were put into place in 2005 to make bankruptcy very difficult for most people to obtain. Prior to the legislation which disallowed most people from walking away from their debts with a court filing, bankruptcies were running at about 1.5 million. The 2005 laws have forced most filers into a structured payment plan, and had been effective in stemming the tide of filings; but now those numbers are going up.

So, despite my sincerest hopes that most consumers will become more in tune with their debt obligations and develop an awareness of the options they have with regard to managing debt problems when they arise, it is obvious that over the next year bankruptcy is still on the horizon for a whopping one million families. Knowing that, it becomes mission critical for every consumer to develop a deeper understanding of bankruptcy, how it affects the credit scores, and how to rebuild after a bankruptcy. Please be aware that bankruptcy is a very involved subject. This book focuses on bankruptcy from a credit perspective and should not be used as a how-to-guide for bankruptcy filings. There are plenty of great books on that subject.

The most common bankruptcies are Chapter 7 and Chapter 13. Here are the differences:

- **Chapter 7** – In this type of bankruptcy, you are asking for the court to discharge all of your debts. It is sometimes referred to as "straight bankruptcy." A Chapter 7 trustee is appointed to take over your property. Any property of value will be sold or turned into money to pay your creditors. Depending on the law of the State in which you file, you may be able to keep some of your personal and real property. If you have the ability to repay your debts, after taking into account reasonable and necessary living expenses, you may not qualify for relief under Chapter 7.

- **Chapter 13** – In this type of bankruptcy you have 3-5 years to pay off your debt and you will be allowed to keep your most valuable property such as your home and your car, but you must earn wages or have some other source of regular income to be a debtor under this chapter. It is frequently referred to as the "wage earner" chapter. The Court must approve your repayment plan and budget. A Chapter 13 trustee is appointed, and will collect the payments from you. The trustee, in turn, will pay your creditors and monitor your compliance with the terms of your repayment plan. After completion of all payments under your plan, you will receive your discharge.

What You Should Know About Bankruptcy Law

Over-extending ourselves financially is not new news. In fact, bankruptcy has a long and colorful history. Bankruptcy protection, in some form, has been around since medieval times. Leave it to the king known for excess and self-indulgence, King Henry VIII, to be the one responsible for passing the first official bankruptcy law in 1542. Under this law, debtors were considered criminals. In 1570, an amendment was made to the law which allowed for the punitive (and painful) provision of severing off an ear as punishment for the crime of bankruptcy, a miserable fate to be certain, but not quite as punishing as being married to King Henry and suffering his disappointment which largely resulted in finding oneself separated from her head.

In the U.S., the first real Bankruptcy Act was passed in 1898 and remained on the books for 80 years. There have been a couple of amendments since then, with the most recent, in 2005, as the most noteworthy. Understanding the changes to the law from a credit perspective will help you understand your options and the differences between them.

The Bankruptcy Abuse Prevention and Consumer Protection Act of 2005

The sweeping overhaul to the bankruptcy code made filing for bankruptcy more difficult. The law virtually doubled the fees associated with bankruptcy and offered significantly less for those fees by adding an increased burden of proving financial hardship. Basically, if you live above the poverty level, your bankruptcy plan will be turned into a payment plan.

The same people who helped get you into this mess are the same people who fought hard for its passage. You guessed it! The credit card companies. They sought to handcuff consumers into debt by forcing a payment plan to amortize the obligation rather than erasing it. I know that in a perfect world, debtors would and should pay for their purchases. But, in my line of work, I have seen that certain hardships challenge an individual's ability to pay. People all too often resort to bankruptcy because of debt burdens that result from a job loss, divorce, or an illness that impairs their ability to service that debt. In fact, during stressful times borrowers lean more heavily on their credit than ever before.

So, especially in light of the revised law, you should understand that there's no escaping financial obligations, and it's really important for you to know your options if and when the "unthinkable" happens to you.

Key Changes To The Bankruptcy Law

- **"Fresh Start" or Chapter 7 debt elimination bankruptcy has become all but impossible.** A core feature is a means test, designed to steer more people toward Chapter 13 bankruptcy, in which they refinance their debt to creditors and pay over a 5-year period of time. If their household incomes are higher than their states' median incomes and they're able to pay $6,000 over 5 years, or about $100 a month, they have to go into Chapter 13 and face a court-imposed debt repayment plan.

- **The new law eliminates the the Judge's discretion to approve or deny a bankruptcy petition.** A "by the numbers" determination is made almost exclusively by a litmus test as to whether the petitioner rests above or below the median income level for the petitioner's state of residence.

- **Lawyers' fees have gone up.** Attorneys now have to ensure accurate filings or face penalties if the petitions contain incorrect information about their clients' finances, and those expenses for the extra time involved are now passed onto the client.

- **If filing under Chapter 13**, a judge, using a formula developed by the Internal Revenue Service, determines how much income can be used for living costs. The rest goes to creditors, generally for a 5-year period. Judging by the two-thirds dropout rate of debtors who try to navigate Chapter 13, it can be a grueling financial workout.

- **People must get credit counseling before filing.** A move that may help some avoid bankruptcy, and no one can exit bankruptcy without taking a course in managing finances.

- **Certain types of debt**, such as some education loans, cannot be erased through bankruptcy.

- **An individual can file under Chapter 7 only once in eight years** (up from 6 years).

The new requirements have forced many potential bankruptcy filers to go underground as the benefits of filing a Chapter 7 fresh start debt elimination have basically become extinct. As protection is scarce and impositions are great, many would-be filers become discouraged by the law's stringency. The ranks of those who attempt to "hide" from creditors will increase. On a positive note, many may achieve greater financial discipline. This is the ideal.

This is a very basic update on the Bankruptcy Law. You can read the entire contents of this new legislation at http://www.uscourts.gov/bankrupt-cycourts/abuseprotection.pdf.

If you find yourself in the position of having to file for bankruptcy, I highly recommend that you do your research on the different types of filings and requirements. A great source for this is the U.S. Bankruptcy Courts site: http://www.uscourts.gov.

How Does A Bankruptcy Affect Credit?

A bankruptcy is reported on your credit report as a public record, and there is no doubt that your scores will drop anywhere from 100-300 points when it first hits, depending on how many points you still have to lose in your payment history factor. Keep in mind, by the time you have filed bankruptcy your scores have already taken a serious hit from the delinquent accounts. That's the bad news. The good news is that you can start rebuilding immediately.

How Long Will A Bankruptcy Remain On Your Credit Report?

Section 605 of the Fair Credit reporting Act states that bankruptcies can remain on a credit report for up to 10 years. Here's the language:

605. Requirements relating to information contained in consumer reports [15 U.S.C. §1681c]

(1) Cases under title 11 [United States Code] or under the Bankruptcy Act that, from the date of entry of the order for relief or the date of adjudication, as the case may be, antedate the report by more than 10 years.

That legal language states that no bankruptcy can be reported for longer than 10 years; however, all three credit bureaus report as follows: Chapter 7 bankruptcies for 10 years from the date of the filing, and Chapter 13 bankruptcies for 7 years, also from the date of filing.

That does not mean that you have to wait 7-10 years to seek removal. I've said it before—to my knowledge there is no language in the law that states items MUST be reported for a certain period of time, only that they CAN be.

Steps For Recovering & Rebuilding Credit After Bankruptcy

> **FACT**
>
> I have reviewed more than 14,000 credit-challenged cases and have NEVER seen a single bankruptcy reported accurately.

Very often, individuals suffer an emotional surrender when they resort to bankruptcy. Frequently they just abandon concerns regarding their credit reports and scores, certain that they face a long and painful road back.

This, absolutely, does not have to be the case. You can embark on your path to recovery from bankruptcy immediately after filing. Doing so will help you emerge from bankruptcy stronger and faster. It will also give you a huge emotional boost because you will feel proactive as opposed to resigned.

- **Pre-Bankruptcy.** As soon as you have decided to file bankruptcy, pull your credit reports and scores. You should clean up any inaccurate or outdated derogatory information before the file goes to bankruptcy. Specifically, you want to validate all delinquency dates on the accounts you will be including—specifically collection accounts. If the 7-Year Reporting Period is around the corner or has already passed, you do not want to include that account in the bankruptcy filing. It will only obligate you to either pay it through a Chapter 13, or may extend the overall reporting period of that account on your credit reports.

  If you are proactive in cleaning up your credit reports prior to filing for bankruptcy, it will lessen the score penalty when the bankruptcy hits. I've seen many credit scores in the mid to high 600s within six months to a year after a bankruptcy has been filed and that is because the rest of the credit was strong. Start as far in advance as you possibly can. Don't make the mistake of assuming that the bankruptcy will take care of everything in the file; it won't.

- **Bankruptcy Re-List.** Don't rely on your attorney to clean up the mess. It's not their job. The strongest tool you have to rebuild after a bankruptcy is through a bankruptcy re-list.

This is a very simple, mission-critical process. Once your bank-ruptcy has been filed, a bankruptcy re-list requires that you go line by line through your credit report to make sure that all items are reported as "included in bankruptcy," listed with a $0 balance. This is very important because it draws a line around the disaster. The credit scoring system has been programmed to understand that there is a containment plan in place and that the items listed in the bankruptcy have been dealt with.

The credit score penalty for a bankruptcy supersedes all other rat-ings on each account included. So if the accounts included are not showing as included, you will be receiving multiple penalties where you should be receiving only one big penalty.

Plus, if accounts are still showing as open, in collection with a bal-ance, collection agencies will continue to try and collect; making your life miserable.

I have seen hundreds of instances in which a bankruptcy re-list has improved consumer credit scores by 50 or more points instantly. If you do not have the energy to conduct the re-list on your own, hire a professional credit repair company to act on your behalf. But this is one step you cannot overlook.

•   **Get a Secured Credit Card**. Do not fall prey to scams. There are many creditors out there who focus specifically on people who have just been through bankruptcy. They see them as easy targets be-cause they know consumers automatically assume they will not be able to get any credit. Stick to a safe plan and apply for a secured credit card within 4-6 months. Then, apply for another secured card within 2-3 months after that. Remember to follow the credit card rules that we discuss in detail in Chapter 7.

•   **Own It.** It's very important that you take full ownership of your long-term credit situation. The court and the lawyers will get you through the bankruptcy, but that's all they will do for you. They will do nothing for your credit recovery, no matter what your law-yer tells you. You need to manage your credit perfectly to get the attention of the scoring system. And that means being vigilant and being consistent. Pull your credit reports every 4-6 months. Re-establish credit steadily, pay on time, keep balances low, and watch your credit for that 80% chance of error that has nothing to do with you. Use the knowledge you have gained from this book.

THE REAL DEAL

The decision to file for bankruptcy is an extremely personal one. The decision requires weighing many conditions; both financial and personal. In the course of this book I cannot possibly describe the many financial, emotional, and personal considerations that factor into the ultimate decision whether or not to file for bankruptcy. What I have tried to do, however, is to show you some reasonable strategies to circumvent a filing, and to recover should bankruptcy be the chosen debt relief option.

Once you do choose the course of action that seems right for you, please realize that this book is only the first step toward guiding you through your credit issues. If you need further assistance regarding bankruptcy, or other important credit issues, please visit my company website at http://www.creditresourcecorp.com. You will find a wealth of information that is likely pertinent to your situation.

[1]http://www.uscourts.gov/bnkrpctystats/statistics.htm

CHAPTER 17

Public & Other Records

Public records are tax liens or judgments that are a part of your public persona. They are very easy to find and very destructive to your reports and scores. Public records, especially when new, can take a huge bite out of your credit scores. In fact, depending on how many points you have to lose, new public records can cost 100-300 points.

The odd little fact about public records is that the amounts of the balances or the judgments do not make a difference in the score. For example, I've seen a client pay $140,000 tax lien in a desperate attempt to get his scores up, and he gained only 10 points. The key to handling all public records is to avoid them at all costs. Validate all public records before paying them. If they are valid, pay them as soon as you can. Remember this one important point: Until public records are paid, you cannot seek early removal.

An important caveat regarding public records: state laws govern them, so it's very important to understand the laws that govern your state and very important to work within those laws.

The Cold Hard Facts About Public Records & Credit

- Having a public record reported on your credit report can drop your credit scores 100-150 points immediately. In the instance of a bankruptcy, this point loss can go up to 300 points.

- When it comes to public records, there is no difference to the credit scoring system of whether or not the item has been paid. I've seen many hundreds of thousands of dollars paid in tax liens that have resulted in a minimal 10-15 point increase in the score.

- Paid or not, public records can stop consumers from getting a job, especially an executive position or a position that is finance related in any way. It can also stop consumers from being approved for business licenses and surety bonds.

- Public records are governed by state statutes. In one state a tax lien may remain on your credit report for up to 15 years, while in another it may remain for 7 years from the date paid. Same applies to judgments. This can make it difficult to have a solid rebuild plan.

- Credit bureaus collect public information from the court directly. Creditors do not report public records.

- The greatest difficulty with public records is that they are court documents. If a consumer discovers a tax lien or judgment erroneously reported on his or her reports, without a court order it is almost impossible to get that item removed; and this means preparing a case and taking it to court.

How Long Do Public Records Remain On A Credit Report

We've touched on this in various chapters, but to keep the subject organized for this chapter, following is the standard credit bureau reporting time for public records. Remember, state rules apply, so the time allowed for reporting may vary. Always check your State Attorney General's site for informaton about your state:

- Paid tax liens remain on file for 7 years from the date paid, or released.

- Unpaid tax liens can remain indefinitely. It depends on state law. Example: In California, unpaid tax liens remain for 10 years.

- Judgments remain on file for 7 years from the date of entry—meaning date filed, or, until the governing statute of limitations has expired. Whichever is the longer period of time. (See Chapter 14.)

- Bankruptcies may be reported for 10 years from the date of filing. However, as discussed in Chapter 16, it is customary for Chapter 13 bankruptcies to be removed after only 7 years.

Tips On Dealing With Public Records

1. As noted, once you have been made aware of a public record on your credit reports, make sure that you validate the record with the credit bureaus. Through the Fair Credit Reporting Act, it is your right and responsibility to verify items on your credit report. Since public records are passed from courthouses to government clerks to credit bureaus, you can usually count on errors creeping in. As a result, the chance of the file being unverifiable is very strong. Given the sheer volume of records and the number of consumers who dispute, you stand a very good chance of having the item removed, especially if it is more than 2-3 years old.

2. If your public records are paid or satisfied, make sure that your credit reports reflect this and that the all dates relating to the tradeline are being reported accurately. As soon as you pay off a public record, you must take the initiative to get the appropriate proof of payment and then send that proof to the credit bureaus that are reporting the item on your credit report. Don't wait! Credit bureaus are notorious for not updating public records when they are paid, and you cannot rely on the court system to update your credit records for you. If they do, it takes months.

3. Make sure your public records are not being reported twice. Because of case numbers, document numbers, court numbers, I've seen many public records reported under two different tradelines, resulting in a DOUBLE PENALTY.

4. Make sure amounts are reported accurately. Although the scoring system does not consider dollar amounts, lenders do.

5. Negotiate. Public records leave consumers vulnerable to garnishments; creditors coming after assets—a constant, stressful, burden of worry. If you have a tax lien or judgment against you that is sitting there because you cannot afford to pay it, negotiate it. Everything is negotiable. You can negotiate an "Offer in Compromise" (OIC) with the IRS to reduce the amount you owe, and you can also negotiate with the creditor or individual who has won a judgment against you. Take action.

Other Significant Records

Felonies

In my experience, I have never seen a felony or conviction reported on a credit report, and I have worked with many individuals with these types of records against them. My opinion is that they are not reported—period. However, the Fair Credit Reporting Act does allow for inclusion of these records on a credit report for 7 years or more, again depending on state law.

If you find yourself in a position of having to re-establish your credit history after a felony or conviction, it is essential that you read this entire book, giving extra attention to the "What If You Don't Have Credit" section in Chapter 22. Take it slowly and it will all come together in good time.

Repossessions

Repossessions are considered the same as a charge-off or collection to the credit scoring system; meaning that you will lose up to 100 points or more once the item is reported, however, the bigger loss here is how employers and lenders look at a repossesion.

If you have a repossession on your credit reports with a balance due, use the tips in Chapter 18 to validate the debt. You'd be surprised at how many auto lenders go out of business, and if that is the case, then validation documents will not be available, and the item will have to be removed.

On the other hand, if the item is validated, see Chapter 15 for some great tips on negotiating for pennies on the dollar in exchange for a deletion letter. If a deletion is not an option, an acceptable alternative would be for the creditor to change the rating on the account from Repossession to Paid Settlement.

Child Support Issues

Any child support that goes unpaid can now be reported on your credit reports, just like a credit card account that you're paying late on. As you know, one 30-day late is a big penalty, plus any amount that you are behind which is listed in the past due column also hurts your credit scores. Remember, child support is court ordered; so if you are not paying your child support because you disagree with the amount, the way to handle it is not by trashing your credit scores. Go to court. Ask for changes—but pay it on time. The courts cannot go back and remove derogatory late pays from your credit report.

However, if you can prove that there was an error in the amount being reported on your credit report and the amount that you have been ordered by the court to pay, then you can dispute the item and it should be fairly easy to have the lates removed.

Student Loans

Student loans are different from unsecured or un-collateralized loans. Student loans have no statute of limitations, are not easily discharged in bankruptcy. The 7-year clock can also be renewed on student loans if the individual reenters into a repayment plan after defaulting on a loan and subsequently goes into default again.

The good news is that in my experience the credit scoring system is more lenient on defaulted student loan accounts; however, these defaults still hurt your credit scores. If your student loans are delinquent or in default, you have many options available; all of which are a positive to credit scores because they stop the delinquency.

1. **Deferment.** This option allows you to "defer" your payments, and halts the interest charge until you are able to repay the debt. Some typical reasons are unemployment, severe financial hardship, temporary disability, or part time study.

2. **Consolidation.** If you have several loans with high interest rates, you can apply for a consolidation loan. This process can put all of your separate loans into one.

3. **Loan Rehab.** Loan Rehab is an option that promises to remove prior delinquency history from a student's credit report upon either completion of the rehabilitaion program or after a certain period of time, such as 9 or 12 months. Unfortunately, in many instances the delinquency is not deleted as promised; thus it's very important to make sure you first get all agreements for deletion and time periods in writing.

4. **Forbearance.** While forbearance does not cease the interest due it does allow breathing room for those who cannot qualify for rehab

or deferment. This option usually allows you to put the loan on hold or reduce the size of your monthly payments.

I recommend that prior to entering into any of the above options, you first speak with your school or current lender to see what programs are available.

ChexSystems

ChexSystems is a service that keeps track of negative information regarding checking and savings accounts. Negative information usually consists of NSF (non-sufficient funds), also known as bouncing checks, or unpaid overdrafts.

A negative ChexSystems report stays in the database for 5 years. Yet being reported to ChexSystems does not currently hurt your credit scores; it does, however, stop any chances of getting a checking account for that period.

To get out of ChexSystems, visit their website at http://www.chexhelp.com.

THE REAL DEAL

These types of records can be devastating to credit reports. They linger much longer than other records and their impact is far more severe. Thus it is best to do everything in your power to avoid having public records reported in your credit history.

If unavoidable, however, the best advice I can give you regarding public and other serious records as outlined above is to be proactive. The minute that you receive indication that a judgment or lien will be filed against you, or that you find out you've been added to ChexSystems, deal with it immediately. Even if you can't afford to pay it, don't ignore it. You will be surprised at how often you can make an arrangement that will keep the file from going to court. That should always be the goal.

CHAPTER 18

The Low Down On Collections

Credit collections weigh very heavy on consumers. In fact, most consumers are so repelled by the entire collections experience that they simply pay them in an effort to end the ongoing harassment. Collection agents count on this, and use intimidation techniques to induce payment. Such intimidation tactics can also cause some consumers to be pushed beyond their own personal point of sanity. In July 2008, The Star Ledger reported that a Newark, New Jersey man was pushed too far by collection agents representing Rent-A-Center Stores. Taking matters into his own hands, a 62-year-old man named Emilio entered the Bloomfield Rent-A-Center location in New Jersey and requested to speak with a supervisor about the non-stop collection calls he was receiving. When a manager was not available, he doused himself in lighter fluid and set himself on fire.

Clearly, this man suffered from some sort of emotional instability, but this 62-year-old man was pushed over the edge by ongoing demands for payment. When he attempted to speak with someone to discuss his concerns, he was unable to do so, and he took extreme measures to make himself heard and—one way or the other—to stop the harassment.

Just how low do collection agents go? You never want to learn the answer to that question firsthand. As a group, they've been reputed to be several levels below the proverbial pond scum. Harassing phone calls at work. Illegal withdrawals from bank accounts. Sometimes even threats of violence or the destruction of your credit and your good name.

Debt collectors make a practice of aggressively attacking those who do not even owe debts. Victims of identity theft or people with a name or social security number similar to the person who really owes the debt are frequently the focus of attacks. And the worst part, consumers pay millions of dollars every year for collections that they don't even owe—just to stop the abuse. Collection agents, well aware that people will do anything to get them off their backs, consider these people "easy pickings."

Worst of all, as discussed in Chapter 2, the fact that these agencies can cause so much damage and chaos without any legal binding agreement with the consumer—to me—is a crime.

Whether you have a debt that slipped through the cracks, unpaid medical bills that should have been paid by your insurance company, a false or expired debt reported on your credit, or a handful of bills you couldn't keep up with five years ago, collections are very damaging to your credit scores and can prevent you from obtaining important credit. The magnitude of collections is so large that it's critical for you to understand how to handle them properly. You need to know how to separate the truth from the myths because, in this case, the obvious solutions may very well be the wrong ones. This chapter provides a significant lesson.

Important Points You Should Know Right Now About Collections

1. **When It Comes To Credit, What Is The Difference Between A Charge Off And A Collection?** A Charge Off is when the creditor writes off the debt to profit and loss on its books. This usually happens after 6 months of non-payment and is strictly for tax purposes. You still owe the money. The collection agency can still (and will) report the account as negative to the credit bureaus, and they may or may not make continued attempts to collect from you. It all depends on the amount owed and whether or not the collection efforts are worth it. When it comes to credit, a charge off and collection are considered the same and should be handled the same. Thus for purposes of this chapter, I'll use the term "Collection."

2. **What Happens To Your Credit Scores When A Debt Goes To Collection?** A single collection can drop your credit scores by as much as 100 points; dealing a devastating blow.

3. **How And When Do Accounts Turn Into Collections?** A debt that goes unpaid for a specified period of time is considered past due.

Each creditor has its own individual policy on how long a bill is past due before they send it to collections. For credit cards, it's usually after you are 120 days past due. For medical and utility bills, it is usually 60-120 days. It varies greatly for other types of accounts. Here are the three most common paths a collection will take:

a) **They Keep It**. Many creditors have their own internal collection department. When an account is seriously past due, the collection department will contact you, requesting that you make payment arrangements. If they are unsuccessful, usually after 6 months, they will "charge off" the debt. The account will be reported on your credit report as a Profit & Loss Write Off, or a Charge Off, with a balance due.

Original creditors are not regulated under the Fair Debt Collection Practices Act. Nonetheless, many state laws regulate their business. Overall, working with the original creditor is less invasive since the internal collection staff is paid on salary as opposed to a commission on the debt they collect. My experience is that if an original creditor keeps the debt, unless the amount owed is exorbitant the serious collection attempts will usually stop within a year, and then pick up again right before the statute of limitations is going to expire. However, the derogatory tradeline will remain until either the 7-Year Reporting Period runs out or until a consumer has it removed through negotiation or dispute.

b) **They Assign It**. If they don't have an internal collection department, some creditors assign the debt to an outside collection agency or a law firm that will pursue collection for a commission. With most creditors, if the initial assignee is not successful in collecting the debt, the original creditor will recall the debt, keep it for 30-60 days, and reassign it to another outside firm. This will go on for many years, sometimes past the expiration date (statute of limitations) of the debt if it has not been paid.

Because the original creditor still owns the debt, you can

communicate with this creditor. This comes in very handy when the account has been sold several times and you have no idea where it is at any given moment. Also, when the debt is still owned by the original creditor, only the creditor, NOT the assigned law firm or the collection agency, is allowed to report the account to the credit bureaus.

c) **They Sell It.** The most common way to handle a collection is for the original creditor to sell the debt directly to a collection agency, for pennies on the dollar. When this happens, communication about the original debt with the original creditor stops completely. The fallout that ensues when the original creditor sells off the debt complicates an already difficult situation. Ongoing turmoil arises when an individual is required to retrace the parties in an attempt to explain the problem and to seek to reconnect the dots to determine what happened and when.

When the debt is sold, the original tradeline should show as a "charge off" with a $0 balance. This is when the problem of multiple collection tradelines for one account begins. When a collection has been sold, it can be sold over and over again, but with a catch, and here it is: Once Collection Agency A sells the debt to Collection Agency B, Collection Agency A should remove its reporting from the credit report because it no longer has the right to collect the debt. However, this doesn't happen without a fight. Without a major battle, collection agencies rarely remove their reporting. This is exactly why consumers pay the same debt over and over again, doing so just to stop the harassment. As you can see, it can turn into a real mess.

Both the Fair Credit Reporting Act and the Fair Debt Collection Practices Act demand accurate reporting from the three major credit bureaus *and* the collection agencies. If a credit bureau continues to report the same collection under multiple tradelines, they can be held liable in a lawsuit. If a collection agency continues to report an item that it does not have the legal right to collect, or reports a collection after the statute has expired, it can also be held liable. This is powerful information for you to know when you are dealing with them.

4. **What Is The Difference Between The Original Creditor And A Collection Agency?** The original creditor is much more difficult to negotiate with than a collection agency. Original creditors don't care about collecting. Original creditors operate on a salary basis, whereas collection agents get paid only when they collect. And, unlike original creditors, a collection agency must comply with the Fair Debt Collection Practices Act. As a result, most consumer strategies to validate and negotiate debt or to cease and desist do not work with the original creditor. Believe it or not, it is actually in your best interest to work with a collection agency because the agency is looking for nothing more than fast cash. And when you begin asserting your rights with demands of validation of debt, you become empowered.

5. **What Happens To Your Credit Scores When You Pay A Collection?** The general rule on how paying collections affects your credit scores is as follows:

    a) If the collection account is *more* than 12 months old, paying it without having it deleted will bring your scores down because it will be reported as a *recent paid collection*. Bottom line: a collection, paid or not, is initially a serious derogatory that can cost a consumer 100 points. However, as time goes on, the penalty ages out; so the older a collection is, the less it hurts your score.

    b) If the collection is *less* than 12 months old, paying it will not hurt your credit scores very much beyond the initial penalty. And in some instances, it may improve your score by a few points. It all depends on the many other elements being reported on your credit report. But my advice is to NEVER pay a collection without first validating the debt, which I will talk about below.

Important Points You Should Know Right Now About Dealing With Collection Agencies

1. **You Can Sue Them And Win!** As we discussed in Chapter 13, it is possible to sue the biggest players in the credit reporting and scoring industry and win. However, the key to winning is knowing your rights and resources that will support your case. Following are three cases wherein major nationwide collection agencies have been sued and ordered to pay for their violations of the laws that protect consumers.

   - **Nationwide Debt Collector Will Pay $1.3 Million to Settle FTC Charges – November 6, 2007**

     A Texas-based debt collection agency will pay more than $1.3 million to settle Federal Trade Commission charges that it misled, threatened, and harassed consumers in violation of federal law.

     "Debt collectors who get complaints from consumers should not only take notice, but also take action," said Lydia B. Parnes, Director of the FTC's Bureau of Consumer Protection. "The message from this case is clear: Either comply with the law or face stiff penalties."

     According to an FTC complaint, in many instances collectors for LTD Financial Services, L.P., which collects on about 1.25 million consumer accounts per year, violated the FTC Act and the Fair Debt Collection Practices Act by falsely threatening or implying that LTD would garnish consumers' wages, seize or attach their property, or initiate lawsuits or criminal actions against them if they failed to pay. *Read more* at http://www.ftc.gov/opa/2007/11/debtcol.shtm.

   - **CAMCO To Pay $1 Million to Settle Unfair, Deceptive Debt Collection Practices – December 5, 2006**

     Capital Acquisitions and Management Corp. and affiliated companies will pay $1 million to settle Federal Trade Commission charges that their debt collection practices violated federal law. The settlement bans the companies from engaging in any future debt collection activities. Previous settlements with eight CAMCO principals and managers also imposed lifetime bans on any future debt collection activities.

In March, 2004, the FTC charged CAMCO, RM Financial, and their principals with threatening and harassing thousands of consumers to get them to pay old, unenforceable debts or debts they did not even owe. The agency alleged that the abusive and deceptive collection practices violated federal law, including the Fair Debt Collection Practices Act. The companies and individuals paid a $300,000 civil penalty to settle the charges and were barred from engaging in abusive, deceptive, and illegal collection practices in the future. *Read more* at http://www. ftc.gov/opa/2006/12/camco.shtm.

- **NCO Group to Pay Largest FCRA Civil Penalty to Date**

One of the nation's largest debt collection firms will pay $1.5 million to settle Federal Trade Commission charges that the firm violated the Fair Credit Reporting Act (FCRA) by reporting inaccurate information about consumer accounts to credit bureaus. The civil penalty against Pennsylvania-based NCO Group, Inc. is the largest civil penalty ever obtained in a FCRA case.

According to the FTC's complaint, defendants NCO Group, Inc.; NCO Financial Systems, Inc.; and NCO Portfolio Management, Inc. violated Section 623(a)(5) of the FCRA, which specifies that any entity that reports information to credit bureaus about a delinquent consumer account that has been placed for collection or written off must report the actual month and year the account first became delinquent. In turn, this date is used by the credit bureaus to measure the maximum 7-Year Reporting Period the FCRA mandates. The provision helps ensure that outdated debts—debts that are beyond this 7-Year Reporting Period—do not appear on a consumer's credit report. Violations of this provision of the FCRA are subject to civil penalties of $2,500 per violation. *Read more* at http://www.ftc.gov/opa/2004/05/ncogroup.shtm.

If you are considering a suit against a collection agency, the best place to gather information on cases pertinent to your cause is http://www.ftc.gov/opa. The information provided there can prove invaluable when you embark on a dispute with a collection agency. When you search the site, look for lawsuits filed against the company you are disputing. Attach that information to your dispute letters. They will know that you are doing your homework and are aware of the fact that you can win.

2.   **What To Do Before Pursing Legal Action**. As discussed above, collections are sold over and over; meaning that in many instances the same collection is reported on a credit report under different names, account numbers, and amounts. Inevitably, once a collection agency sells the debt to another, the agency fails to remove its reporting from the credit report. This is illegal, yet happens all the time. For this reason, I always advise my clients to first dispute the account with the credit bureaus before pursing more in-depth solutions. This way, any items that don't belong on the report will be removed. Doing so will save you much time in pursing dispute activity with collection agencies or creditors who 1) don't exist anymore, or 2) don't have your records on file anymore. Once you have done so, you will be able to focus on the real source of the problem rather than chasing down phantoms that drain your time and resources.

WORD OF CAUTION

Remember, many creditors do not report to all three credit bureaus; so be sure to only dispute a derogatory item to the credit bureau that is reporting that item. Otherwise you risk having that negative item added to the reports that are not currently showing them.

3. **Collection Agency Business Licenses Get Suspended All the Time!** Learn as much as you can about the collection agency. In many instances, you will find:

   a) The collection agency is not licensed to operate in the state in which it is trying to collect; and/or

   b) The collection agency has a suspended license, a very common occurrence.

If either of these is the case, the collection agency cannot collect on the debt and you can request removal from the credit bureaus reporting the item. Better yet, you can sue the collection agency for attempting to collect under false circumstances.

Licensing is generally handled through your state. The U.S. Small Business Administration Office has gathered links to all state offices handling Business Licensing. This would be a good place to start your research: http://www.sba.gov/hotlist/license.html.

4. **Collection Agencies Report Assigned Accounts All The Time!** As outlined above, a collection agency can only report to the credit bureaus if it *owns* the debt; however, many still report the debt even if the debt has been assigned elsewhere.

Before entering into negotiations with a collection agency, you want to call the original creditor first to make sure that the creditor has SOLD—not merely assigned the rights—to the collection agency. If you find that the agency is reporting a collection that has been assigned, not sold, you can send a letter notifying the agency that you will pursue legal action if they do not remove the account from your credit reports. Also be sure to send a copy of that letter to each of the credit bureaus reporting the account.

5. **NEVER Let Your Guard Down — They Will Annihilate.** Collection agents are trained to look for consumer weakness and then to pounce on that weakness. During your very first conversation with a collector, whether the agent is calling you or you are calling the agent, try to remember the following:

   a) Assume that you should not believe anything the agent

says. He or she will do and say anything to get you to pay the debt right then and there.

b) Remember, you will always catch more flies with honey than with vinegar, so make sure that you are completely relaxed and calm when you make the call. The collection agent will do everything possible to upset you and put you on the defensive. Don't fall for it! Let the collector think that you are having this conversation because you want to rectify the situation, and that you are not even sure if it is your debt. Ask this individual to send you something to jar your memory. Your goal is to get the company name and address so that you can send a letter asking for validation of the agent's claim.

c) NEVER tell them your story until *after* they have fully validated the debt and you want to start negotiating.

d) Immediately ask that they "please" not call you on the number in their database. When asked what number they can call you on, explain that there is no number. Ask them to send all communication in writing. By law, they must oblige.

6. **A Good Faith Payment—It's A Trap!** In Chapter 14, I talk about the difference between the 7-Year Reporting Period and the Statute of Limitations on debt collection. Now you know that if you make a payment on an expired debt or if you make a written or oral promise to pay it, you may renew the statute and it will be irreversible unless you can prove that you were misled by the collection agent.

Once the debt has "expired," negotiations with the collection agency can pay off. By being proactive you can have the item removed, and for pennies on the dollar. You can do so by advising the creditor that the statute of limitations has run out, but that you would be willing to pay 20-30 cents on the dollar for full deletion.

WORD OF CAUTION

Sometimes original creditors will allow a collection account to sit dormant until 6 months before the statute of limitations will expire. Then they either assign it or sell it to a collection agency that will aggressively try to collect the debt because the collector knows the statute is about to expire. This is why many consumers don't hear about collections for years; and then suddenly, out of nowhere, they are hit hard with collection efforts.

7. **Never Send Money Without A Written Agreement—Never!** First of all, unless you are 100% certain that the claim is accurate all the way, never agree to pay any collection debt without validating it first. Whether you have agreed to enter into a payment plan, or to settle the debt for less as *payment in full*, NEVER send money until you have a written agreement from the collection agency that clearly outlines the terms of the agreement. It's as simple as the company sending you an email or a faxed letter on its letterhead stating that "If you pay $____ by January 1, 2008, ABC Collection Agency will accept that amount as payment in full for Bank of XYZ Account Number 123456, and ABC Collection Agency will delete the account from the three major credit reporting agencies: Equifax, Experian and TransUnion."

If the collection agent says he or she cannot give you an agreement in writing before payment is made, then HANG UP THE PHONE, and call back to speak with a supervisor. Don't sign anything or make any promises to pay the debt until the creditor or collection agency first presents you with an agreement in writing.

WORD OF CAUTION

Remember, dollar amount doesn't matter. Do not make the mistake of thinking that it's not necessary to validate debts or get agreements in writing just because the amount of the debt is small. The score penalty does not differntiate between $100 collection and and $10,000 collection.

8. **Beware of Tricky Language—Update Does Not Mean Delete!** When negotiating a payoff agreement with a collection agency, best-case scenario is to ALWAYS negotiate deletion in exchange for payment. If you DO get them to agree to a deletion, get it in writing; but, be careful, because they will try to trick you. They may say "yes, we will make sure to update this information to the credit reporting agencies." This is misleading. When they say *update*, what they really mean is that they will update the account to a paid collection, and this will, as you now know, drop your scores. If you are successful in negotiating the deletion, the agreement must say DELETE, not update.

9. **Do Not Believe Their Legal Threats Until You are Served.** Many collection agencies make false legal threats leading consumers to believe that papers have been filed. You can sue them for this. Go back and review Chapter 13, under the Fair Debt Collection Practices Act.

10. **Ask For A Supervisor**—If, during a phone call with a collection agency you feel that the tables have turned and the conversation is no longer going your way, politely tell the person you are speaking with that you appreciate his or her time but would like to speak with a supervisor. In most instances, the individual will tell you that there is no supervisor and will not pass you through. When this happens, hang up and call back. Explain to the person on the other end that you just had a very unpleasant experience with the agent handling your file, and would like to speak with a supervisor. If you are persistent, you will get through.

Review Your Rights — You Have Plenty Of Them When It Comes To Collections

As outlined in Chapter 13, The Fair Debt Collection Practices Act (FDCPA), 15 U.S.C.1692 is a federal statute that prohibits a debt collector from using certain collection methods in an attempt to collect a debt. I advise that you to go back and review this chapter if you find yourself in a position of disagreement with a collection agency about its methods of trying to collect and report a debt. You should also take some time to read a summary of this Act at http://www.ftc.gov/bcp/edu/pubs/consumer/credit/cre27.pdf.

People fail to meet their credit obligations for a variety of reasons. These reasons can range from over-extension of finances to unemployment and illness. Whatever the reason, every person is protected by the Fair Debt Collection Practices Act.

Validation Of Debt (VOD) – A Powerful Tool

Validation of Debt (VOD) is the single greatest tool you can use to deal with collectors, and, unless you are 100% certain that the account is being reported accurately, VOD should be used before paying or negotiating a payoff for any charge-off or collection. Remember, statistics show that 80% of consumer credit reports contain errors!

Here's the code from the Fair Debt Collection Practices Act.

§ 809. Validation of debts (Title 15, Chapter 41, Sec. 1692g)

(a) **Notice of debt** — *Within five days after the initial communication with a consumer in connection with the collection of any debt, a debt collector shall,* unless the following information is contained in the initial communication or the consumer has paid the debt, send the consumer a written notice containing -

(1) the amount of the debt;

(2) the name of the creditor to whom the debt is owed;

(3) a statement that *unless the consumer, within 30 days after receipt of the notice, disputes the validity of the debt,* or any portion thereof, the debt will be assumed to be valid by the debt collector;

(4) a statement that *if the consumer notifies the debt collector in writing within the 30-day period* that the debt, or any portion thereof, is disputed, the debt collector will obtain *verification of the debt* or a copy of a judgment against the consumer and a copy of such verification or judgment will be mailed to the consumer by the debt collector; and

(5) a statement that, *upon the consumer's written request within the 30-day period,* the debt collector will provide the con-

201

sumer with the name and address of the original creditor, if different from the current creditor.

(b) **Disputed debts** — If the *consumer notifies the debt collector in writing within the 30-day period* described in subsection (a) of this section that the debt, or any portion thereof, is disputed, or that the consumer requests the name and address of the original creditor, *the debt collector shall cease collection of the debt, or any disputed portion thereof, until the debt collector obtains verification of the debt* or a copy of a judgment, or the name and address of the original creditor, *and a copy of such verification* or judgment, or name and address of the original creditor, *is mailed to the consumer by the debt collector.*

(c) **Admission of liability** — *The failure of a consumer to dispute the validity of a debt under this section may NOT be construed by any court as an admission of liability by the consumer.*

This means that you have 30 days from the time a collection agency contacts you to ask that certain documentation be provided by the collection agency to validate the debt. If the agency cannot validate the debt, then it must remove the debt from your credit report. However, it is never that simple.

Here's What You Need To Know About VOD

If you've ever tried to validate a debt with a collection agency or creditor, then you already know it's like pulling teeth to get the agency to produce valid documentation proving its claim. The collection agency or creditor will send you a statement printed on a computer system, or a copy of your original agreement with a credit card company, but I've seen very few cases when a collection agency produces substantial verification as required by law.

Why? Because the law under Title 15 of the US Code is not clear on the definition of what documents constitute "Verification." However, after doing my research I found that Title 42, Chapter 77, Subchapter IV, Part A, Section 6381 does in fact define the term "Verification" as follows: Verification Examination means: Examination of such books, records, papers, or other documents of a person or company necessary and appropriate to assess the accuracy, reliability, and adequacy of the information, or financial information. I have a feeling that if I took a year to read the entire code, I would find more crossover definitions that would apply.

I believe the definition of "Verification" in one title of the US Code should apply in all titles, in its general meaning.

The dictionary definition of "verify" supports this assumption:

- Verify: 1) to confirm or substantiate in law by oath; 2) to establish the truth, accuracy, or reality of

- Additionally, the Thesaurus results for "verify" are as follows: confirmation, substantiation, proof, evidence, and authentication.

In all cases, the term verification suggests the process of providing proof or evidence. This code provides you with a powerful tool for request of production of materials that provide proof of claim. This is precisely what the credit bureaus require of consumers when they seek to have items removed from their reports. Request for verification turns the tables on this requirement, putting you back in the driver's seat by forcing them to either prove the debt, or get rid of it.

Send A Validation Of Debt Letter Immediately

Many consumers undergo an internal struggle trying to do the right thing when it comes to paying their debts, and I commend them; however, my advice to you is that if you are not 100% certain that everything about that account is being reported true and accurate, then a Validation of Debt letter should be sent immediately. You can always make a payment offer at a later date.

True and accurate means:

- The debt belongs to you.

- The Statute on collecting the debt has NOT expired.

- The amount being collected is accurate and fair. Some companies illegally try to collect unethical amounts of interest and penalties.

- The date of last activity on that account (date of original creditor default) is accurate. A 2002 collection being reported with a Date of Last Activity of 2007 is NOT accurate.

- If it is an older collection, the fact that you may have already paid another collection agency or the original creditor is a possibility.

The point is that it is almost impossible to say that a collection account is being reported 100% accurately unless you have kept all records pertaining to that account from day one. My advice is to *always* validate collection debt prior to making payment or a promise to pay.

Validation Of Debt Template Letter

Here is a sample Validation of Debt letter:

Date

Collection Agency Name
Address

Re: Original Creditor:
     Account Number:
     Amount:

To Whom It May Concern:

In response to your letter dated _____ (or: your phone call on _____) regarding the above account, please accept this as my formal request for (Collection Agency Name) to produce absolute proof and validation of the said debt under Title 15 of US Code 1692 (g) Section 809 (b) of the Fair Debt Collections Practices Act.

The proof requested is as follows:

- All records pertaining to actual debt to prove that the account belongs to me, including my signature on the original account application

- A statement of all charges to the account adding up to the amount that you are trying to collect, including fees, penalties and interest, separated out in total

- Date of first delinquency with (Original Creditor Name) that led to the collection

- Date that you purchased the debt and proof that you have the right to collect on behalf of (Original Creditor Name)

- Date of last payment/activity if any on the account

- Full name and address of your direct contact at (Original Creditor Name)

(Collection Agency Name) has 30 days to respond with absolute proof as required by law. In addition, if (Collection Agency Name) has not reported this account to the three major credit bureaus, Equifax, Experian, and TransUnion, then (Collection Agency Name), by law, cannot do so now that I am disputing the validity of it's claim. However, if (Collection Agency Name) has already reported the item to the three major credit bureaus, and cannot produce the above-requested absolute proof, then I am requesting that (Collection Agency Name) immediately remove any negative reporting from my credit bureau files at Equifax, Experian and TransUnion as continuing to report an unverifiable, disputed debt on my credit reports would be an FCRA violation.

I have attached a copy of a recent verdict; (lawsuit name) wherein (name of collection agency that was sued) was found in violation of the FDCPA and was forced to pay damages. I am well aware of my consumer credit rights under all Acts, and I reserve the right to file a suit against (Collection Agency Name) for FCRA and FDCPA violations in my court's venue should (Collection Agency Name) not follow the law on this issue.

I am also going to request that you cease from making any further phone calls to my telephone number (your telephone number) as I use this telephone number for business. I am requesting that all future communication from (Collection Agency Name) is by U.S. Mail.

I look forward to your timely response.

Sincerely,

Here are some tips on sending a Validation of Debt Letter:

1. Make sure you send the letter via certified mail, and that you obtain proof of delivery for your file. Keep a copy of the letter and any other communication you have from the collector.

2. Allow the collection agency 30 days to reply, and be sure to review its proof closely because, in most instances, the agency will try to send you everything but what you ask for in your VOD letter. Accept nothing less than absolute proof.

3. At the same time that you send your VOD letter to the collection agency, send a copy of the VOD letter and proof of delivery to the credit bureaus who are reporting the collection, letting them know that you are disputing the validity of the debt. This will start the investigation process at the credit bureau level, and will put the collection agency in a position of potentially violating the FDCPA if they respond to the credit bureaus investigation by verifying the account.

    If you receive a response from the credit bureau that states the collection agency has VERIFIED the validity of the account, be sure to keep that document in the file. You will need it should you be forced to go to court and want to request that the credit bureau prove its verification claim and process.

Sending The VOD Letter In A Timely Manner Is Critical For Two Reasons:

1. If the collection has not been reported yet to the credit bureaus, the collection agency cannot report it once a VOD Letter has been sent. If they do report the collection, it is in violation of the Fair Debt Collection Practices Act and you can sue for damages.

2. Even though the law states that the failure of a consumer to dispute the validity of a debt is not considered admission of liability, it is best to respond as soon as possible. Do not ignore collection notices. If you do not dispute the debt and the collection turns into a judgment, the consequences are much more difficult to repair.

What If The 30 Days Has Passed?

Since collections are sold over and over again, it's almost impossible for consumers to meet this 30-day deadline. And in most instances, people don't even find out about collections until they apply for a loan, or pull their credit, or get a phone call from out the blue.

The law states that you should respond to the collection notice within 30 days, but it does not state that you can't respond later. It's a matter of interpretation. The only thing that can happen is that the collection agency uses the 30-day rule to ignore your requests for validation. However, through my experience I have seen that if consumers are persistent in the process once they start, and build their case by keeping a record of all dispute activity from that date forward, then if the situation does become legal the court will usually require that the collection agency produce the requested validation documents.

Again, in Section 809 of the Fair Credit Debt Collection Practices Act, under **Admission of Liability** as outlined above, the act clearly states that *the fact that a consumer does not dispute the validity of debt does NOT mean they are admitting that they owe the debt.*

Letter Of Intent To Sue The Collection Agency

If you do not hear from the collection agency within 30 days of sending the VOD Letter, you have a choice to make. The next step in the process would be to send the collection agency a letter of intent to sue. However, it is illegal to make such a threat if you do not have the intent to follow through. So it is important to give this option careful consideration before proceeding.

Here are some tips on sending a letter of intent to sue:

1. Make sure that you send the letter via certified mail, and that you obtain proof of delivery for your file.

2. Allow the collection agency 15-20 days to reply.

3. Send a copy of the letter of intent to sue to the credit bureaus that are reporting the collection, with a copy of the original VOD letter and certified receipts for both. Ask the bureaus to remove the item from your credit report immediately, based on the fact that the collection agency has violated the FDCPA by not validating the debt in

question. No need to recite the Acts that have been violated because you will be sending copies of all letters to the bureaus.

File A Small Claims Action

If the collection agency does not respond to your intent to file a suit letter with absolute proof of its claim as it is listed in the VOD Letter, then my advice is to immediately file a lawsuit in small claims court. By this time, you will have proof that the agency has violated the Fair Debt Collection Practices Act in the following ways:

1. They failed to validate the debt when you requested in writing that they do so.

2. Despite their failure to provide validation to you, they told a credit bureau the debt was valid.

3. Lastly, producing your letter of intent to sue, as well as proof of receipt of that letter, will demonstrate they had reasonable time to respond in a manner that is required by furnishers of information under the Fair Debt Collection Practices Act and the Fair Credit Reporting Act.

Small claims court is a quick and low-cost way to resolve civil disputes. A filing in small claims court against the collection agency may prompt a response from them, stating that they will delete the item from your credit reports and stop all collection efforts. Alternatively, the filing may also cause them to stonewall the suit and fail to show up at the hearing, in which case you have an instant judgment in your favor.

By following all of these important steps, and by keeping bulletproof records of all information and correspondence, a judge would be hard-pressed to not rule in your favor.

Once you have prevailed in court, be sure to send copies of every court order document as proof of your judgment and request immediate deletion.

I cannot stress enough the importance of validating debt. It will buy you time; it will get the collectors off your back; it will wipe out debts that are invalid and/or inaccurately reported. However, as noted, it is imperative that you do not make false threats of legal action unless you intend to proceed.

What To Do If The Collection Agency Validates The Debt

If the collection agency responds with valid proof of the debt, don't necessarily pay off the debt right away. I am not suggesting that you not pay your debts. Obviously, you want to be current on all of your bills, unless they are debts that have gone to collections. In this case, it is a matter of how and when to pay your collection debts so that you are not prohibited from getting a loan, and you want to make sure that it brings the least credit score penalty possible. Here are some pointers:

1. If the collection is *less than* 12 months old, as outlined above, paying it will not hurt your credit scores very much in addition to the initial penalty. If you are certain that the debt belongs to you and that the collection agency has the legal right from the original creditor to collect the debt, then my advice is to pay it and put it behind you. If you cannot negotiate a deletion letter, then the best-case scenario is that the account will be updated to paid, and after a year or so, you can seek removal. Remember, there is no law on the books that says derogatory information *must be* reported for 7 years.

2. If the collection is *more than* 12 months old, your options are as follows:

    •   If you cannot afford to pay the debt and you are not being harassed by a collection agency or original creditor for payment, you can just let the item sit on your credit report until the 7-Year Reporting Period has expired, unless you plan to enter into a credit transaction in the near future that requires all collections are paid.

    •   If you can afford to pay the debt, and the statute of limitations has expired, negotiate a payment of 20-30 cents on the dollar in exchange for deletion. Again, if the statute has expired, the collection agency will be more motivated to accept your offer. If not, waiting for the 7-Year Reporting Period to expire is another option.

    •   If you can afford to pay the debt and the statute of limitations has *not* expired, still negotiate for a lesser payment in full and be prepared to be persistent in negotiating a deletion letter or your credit scores can drop by up to 100 points.

- Do not pay an older collection if you are in the middle of a loan transaction. When the lender re-pulls your report at closing, the drop in the credit scores could cause you to lose the loan. In this case, collections should be paid after escrow closes.

  The exception would be if the creditor or collection agency is going to take legal action.

If You Don't Have Time To Go Through The Validation Of Debt Process

I do not recommend paying any collection that hasn't been validated, but the validation process takes time—at minimum 45-60 days. So if you are in a hurry, here are some tips to help you negotiate better terms when paying off older collections:

- If you do not have documents to determine whether or not the Statute of Limitations has expired on a collection debt, go through your files and look for an old credit report. Call a past creditor or mortgage professional who may have kept a copy of your credit report. What you are looking for is evidence of the date of last activity on that account, because if the statute has expired, you can remind the collection agent of that point which will give you a much better negotiating position for a lower pay-off and a deletion letter.

- Go through your old files and look for anything and everything that can be used as proof of your first 30-day late payment that led to the collection or charge off. It could be bank statements showing that you stopped making payments for 2-3 months in a row, or letters from the creditor confirming your delinquency, or credit card statements showing your last charge, or it could even be rejection letters from creditors who denied you based on a particular collection.

- Call the original creditor and request that the creditor send you a copy of your file immediately. If they state that the file is no longer in their possession, THEY ARE LYING. Remind them that they are reporting a negative trade line on your credit report and even though they may have sold the item to a collection agency, per the Fair Credit Reporting Act, they MUST give you a copy of your file or remove the trade line from your reports.

- Finally, beg and plead for deletion. Pride should not be an issue when it comes to saving your credit rating.

Tips On Negotiating With Collection Agencies

- Don't let them know that you are going into a loan transaction. They will be less likely to oblige.

- Start your negotiating mid-month and hold out until the last day. The last day of the month is when collection agents cut off their commission quota.

- Remind them that by law they are not required to report derogatory information to the credit bureaus.

CREDIT TIP

When you are in the position of having to pay a collection that is more than 12 months old, and you cannot negotiate a deletion letter, insist that the credit bureaus, per the Fair Credit Reporting Act, list the original date of delinquency on your credit report, and NOT the date when the item was paid. You can do this by sending them proof. That is why, unless you have absolute proof of this date, it is so important to go through the validation process.

THE REAL DEAL

The best credit advice I can give you when it comes to collections is to always be proactive. It is critical that you stay on top of your bills, financially and organizationally. This way you can prevent ever having to deal with collections. Collections are devastating to your credit scores and they can take you down a path that is uncomfortable, humiliating, time consuming, and extremely frustrating. They are also frequently avoidable.

However, it is also important to understand that strange things do happen in the credit world, and even people with great credit histories can get thrown for a loop. Unresolved medical bills, statements sent to the wrong addresses, bills that are misplaced or mislabeled, an all too clever deviant who steals your identity and manipulates your credit can force collections situations for people with otherwise stellar credit history.

The key to handling collections is to stay on top of every aspect of them. Know the system in terms of which action to take and when. Know when you should walk away and when you should begin negotiating. Most importantly, know the rules that govern collection agents. The FDCPA is a strongly worded Act that provides you with plenty of artillery for a strong counter attack against nervy, unresponsive, and unscrupulous collectors. When you know the laws about collections, you will be able to turn the course to your advantage.

CHAPTER 19

Mortgage & Credit
Can't Refinance It,
Can't Sell It, and
Can't Afford It

What is a short sale and how can it affect my credit?

What about a Deed In Lieu of Foreclosure?

Is it better to file for bankruptcy or to be foreclosed?

What should I do?

Every day, these questions are asked of me by frightened homeowners and mortgage professionals who are quickly trying to respond to the financial chaos that arises from the subprime mortgage fiasco which has touched millions of American homeowners.

Like no other financial crisis this country has seen since the Great Depression, the home lending fiasco has turned the American Dream into the American Nightmare. It has taken down millions of homeowners. It has brought the global financial markets to its knees. And it has catalyzed the implosion of massive banking entities whose greed proved the key to their unraveling.

The mortgage crisis has paralyzed the hopes and futures of millions of homeowners who are now wondering how they will manage their way through the lending crisis. How will they manage their credit through the turbulent economic and financial strangleholds in which they find themselves trapped? Is there relief? Is there any salvaging of the current housing market? What is the best path for consumers to get there?

There's no question that many families will have to leave their homes. Their biggest question now is how to most effectively do so (without devastating their credit scores) so that they will someday be able to buy a home again.

I speak to families every day, and I am heartened by those who have the wisdom and emotional strength to face these tough issues head on! They will be served well by their courage, and their credit scores will be better off for it!

Now is the time for tough questions to be asked and answered.

Note: The guidelines to which I refer in this chapter are the recent selling guidelines of Fannie Mae & Freddie Mac, the two companies (recently taken over by the U.S. government) that own or guarantee about half of the U.S.'s $12 trillion in mortgages. These companies base their decisions to purchase mortgage loans on guidelines that are national policy. These guidelines mandate specific credit requirements and policies with respect to problematic situations such as foreclosure, deed in lieu of foreclosure, short sale, or bankruptcy. Specifically, a demonstration of an impeccable credit history must be shown for a designated period of time after the negative event has occurred.

There Are No Requirements On Mortgage Lenders To Report Negative Information To The Credit Bureaus

When it comes to how a lender will report to the credit bureaus, I bring this to your attention as moral support in consumer efforts to NEGOTIATE, NEGOTIATE, NEGOTIATE.

As discussed in Chapter 2, under the Hardship Flaw, the Fair Credit Reporting Act clearly states that creditors are not required to report negative information to the credit bureaus.

There's more to this story, however. An August 13, 2008 Announcement from Fannie Mae & Freddie Mac clearly states that they place NO requirement on *how* lenders report mortgage default accounts to the credit bureaus. In response to the frequently asked question about how these items should appear on the credit report, the announcement stated: [1]

"For reporting these actions on Fannie Mae loans, we require that servicers report to one of the major credit reporting agencies, *but it is our policy NOT to direct specifically how to report various actions.*"

This is powerful and significant information. If the Fair Credit Reporting Act doesn't require lenders to report negative information at all, or in a specific manner, and the nation's largest buyer of mortgage loans does not require lenders to report negative information at all, or in a specific manner, this leaves the door wide open for negotiating deletions or non-reporting of these items. So I reiterate: NEGOTIATE, NEGOTIATE, NEGOTIATE.

Homeowner Options & How They Affect Credit Scores

Foreclosure, Deed in Lieu of Foreclosure, Short Sale, and Bankruptcy can all have long-lasting impact on an individual's taxes and ability to obtain credit. Homeowners need to get the facts before making critical decisions that will impact their lives for many years to come.

The following is a breakdown of homeowner options, and how each affects the credit scores. There are several loan products available, but, as previously mentioned, Fannie Mae & Freddie Mac own or guarantee about half of the U.S.'s mortgage market, so it is best to use their most recent Selling Guidelines as laid out in their June 25, 2008 Announcement.[2]

Foreclosure

Foreclosure is the legal process by which a bank or other secured creditor either sells or repossesses a parcel of real property, home or land after the owner has failed to comply with the mortgage or deed of trust agreement with the lender. Most frequently, the violation of the mortgage agreement is the default of payment. The completion of the foreclosure process allows the lender to sell the property and keep the proceeds to pay off the mortgage as well as any legal costs. The length of the foreclosure process varies from state to state.

If the foreclosed property is sold for less than the remaining primary mortgage balance, and there is no insurance to cover the loss, the court overseeing the foreclosure process may enter a deficiency judgment against the borrower. Deficiency judgments can be used to place a lien on the borrower's other personal property, obligating the borrower to repay the difference or suffer the loss of one's property. It gives the lender a legal right to collect the remainder of debt out of the borrower's other existing assets.

However, there are exceptions to this rule. If the mortgage is classified as "non-recourse debt," then in the event of foreclosure the borrower has no personal liability. This is often the case with residential mortgages. If so, the lender may not go after the borrower's personal assets to recoup additional loss.

The lender's ability to pursue a deficiency judgment can be restricted by state laws. In California and some other states, original mortgages (the ones taken out at the time of purchase) are typically non-recourse loans; however, refinanced loans and home equity lines of credit are not.

If the lender chooses not to pursue deficiency judgment—or can't, because the mortgage is non-recourse—and writes off the loss, the borrower may have to pay income taxes on the un-repaid amount even if it can be considered "forgiven debt."

Any other loans taken out against the property being foreclosed (second mortgages, home equity lines of credit) are "wiped out" by foreclosure (in the sense that they are no longer attached to the property), but the borrower is still obligated to pay them off if they are not paid out of the foreclosure auction's proceeds.

How Does A Foreclosure Affect Credit?

A foreclosure can be reported as a Foreclosure or Repossession and carries the most negative penalty on a credit score just under a public record (i.e. bankruptcy, tax lien, or judgment.) There is a misconception that foreclosures are considered public records to the scoring system. However, they are not. Although there is a Public Notice Record on file once a foreclosure is started, this record is completely different than a credit report public record.

Unless a foreclosure becomes a public record, such as a judgment, it can only be reported on a credit report for 7½ years from the date of the first late pay that led to foreclosure. Many consumers and lenders believe that it is 7 years from the completion date of the foreclosure process, but that is inaccurate. A foreclosure falls under the same rules as a collection, charge-off, or other similar action. See Chapter 14 under —When Does the 7-Year Reporting Period Start?"

A foreclosure can drop credit scores from 50-250 points (this includes points already lost due to delinquent payments). The difference in point loss depends on how many points someone has to lose in the payment history factor of his or her credit report. Thus if someone has a 750 credit score and they opt to foreclose, their score could drop up to 250 points. However, if someone has a 500 credit score, they may only lose 50 points for the same derogatory.

If a deficiency judgment or tax lien is filed in connection with a foreclosure, credit scores can drop an additional 100 points.

How Long Before You Can Buy Another Home After Foreclosure?

The current guidelines from Fannie Mae & Freddie Mac state that the waiting period for a foreclosure is 5 years from the date the foreclosure proceeding is completed.

However, if extenuating circumstances caused the borrower to enter into a foreclosure proceeding, such as the subprime mortgage crisis fallout, loss of employment or a severe medical crisis, the waiting period, if approved, is 3 years from the date the foreclosure proceeding is completed.

In General: When it comes to foreclosure and how it affects the ability to obtain credit in the future, there are multiple points of extremely negative impact. Deficiency judgments for the amount not collected by the lender in the foreclosure sale can end up on a borrower's credit report as a derogatory mark. Additionally, there is a high risk that the borrower will be hit with a substantial tax penalty which can result in a tax lien which also appears on the credit report. As a general rule, other than a bankruptcy, foreclosure is the least desirable of all of the options available when a borrower is upside down in a home mortgage.

Deed In Lieu Of Foreclosure

One option to foreclosure is a "deed in lieu of foreclosure." In this scenario the borrower turns the house over to the lender and walks away without owing anything. A deed in lieu of foreclosure offers several advantages to both the borrower and the lender. The main advantage to the borrower is that it immediately releases him or her from most or all of the personal debt associated with the defaulted loan. The borrower also avoids a foreclosure proceeding and may receive more generous terms than he or she would obtain in a formal foreclosure. Advantages to a lender include a reduction in the time and cost of repossessing the property.

In most instances, in order to be considered for a deed in lieu of foreclosure the total debt on the property should be secured by the real estate being transferred. Both sides must enter into the transaction *voluntarily* and in *good faith*. The settlement offer must at least be equal to the fair market value of the property being turned over. Generally, the lender will not proceed with a deed in lieu of foreclosure if the outstanding debt on the property exceeds the current fair market value of the property.

Because the agreement must be voluntary, lenders will often not act upon a deed in lieu of foreclosure unless they receive a written offer from the borrower that specifically states that the offer to enter into negotiations is being made voluntarily. This will enact the parole evidence rule and protect the lender from a possible subsequent claim that the lender acted in bad faith or pressured the borrower into the settlement. Both sides may then proceed with settlement negotiations.

Neither the borrower nor the lender is obliged to proceed with the deed in lieu of foreclosure until a final agreement is reached.

How Does A Deed In Lieu Of Foreclosure Affect The Borrower's Credit?

Most lenders report a deed in lieu of foreclosure as a foreclosure, so the credit scores will carry the same serious effect as if it were an actual foreclosure. However, borrowers can negotiate with the lender to report it differently in return for turning over the deed and avoiding foreclosure costs.

Many lenders will say that they cannot change the reporting status, but as you now realize, they can. Here are the credit reporting options in preferred order:

- Paid As Agreed—Credit scores will have already dropped over 100 points due to default in payments; however, if reported as Paid As Agreed, the borrower will be able to purchase another home in a shorter time period.

- Paid Settlement—Credit scores could drop up to 100 points in addition to the points already lost for delinquent payments.

- Foreclosure—See above.

How Long Before You Can Buy Another Home After Deed In Lieu Of Foreclosure?

The current guidelines from Fannie Mae & Freddie Mac state that the waiting period for a Deed in Lieu of Foreclosure is 4 years from the date the proceeding is completed.

If there are extenuating circumstances that caused the borrower to have to enter into a Deed In Lieu of Foreclosure proceeding, the waiting period is 2 years from the date the proceeding is completed.

Short Sale (aka: Pre-Foreclosure Sale)

The best option is a short sale, which occurs when a bank or mortgage lender agrees to discount a loan balance due to an economic hardship on the part of the homeowner. The homeowner sells the mortgaged property for less than the outstanding balance of the loan, and turns over the proceeds of the sale to the lender in full satisfaction of the debt. In such instances, the lender would have the right to approve or disapprove a proposed sale.

A short sale is typically executed to prevent a home foreclosure. Lenders often choose to allow a short sale if they believe that it will result in a smaller financial loss than foreclosing. For the homeowner, the advantages include avoidance of having a foreclosure on their credit history. Additionally, a short sale is typically faster and less expensive than a foreclosure.

How Does A Short Sale Affect The Borrower's Credit?

In the wake of the devastating mortgage crisis of 2008, short sales are becoming extremely common. In fact, a backlog of cases has forced lenders to prioritize their caseloads. This largely means that homeowners have to be in default to get their attention. This is unfortunate, because late pays can cause serious drops in credit scores.

The good news is that borrowers who choose the short sale option show that they are exhausting every effort to pay the loan. The borrower has willingly committed to taking on months of emotional and physical stress in a good-faith effort to sell the property to maintain a good relationship with that lender. Most likely, the borrower or borrowers are unable to pay their current mortgage because they had an adjustable product and their mortgage payment doubled. This type of situation doesn't mean that they can't afford a different loan program with a lower payment. Which leads me to wonder what the incentive is for lenders to report short sales to the credit bureaus. All they would be doing is cutting off a pretty substantial future income stream if they put these types of borrowers out of the market for years. With this in mind, negotiation for a non-report on short sales— and also the removal of late pays due to the lender not being able to process the short sale fast enough—is well worth pursuing and is completely legal!

Here are the credit reporting options in preferred order:

- Paid As Agreed—Won't hurt the score at all as long as the borrower has kept payments current.

- Unrated—May drop a few points.

- Paid Settlement—Credit scores will drop 50-150 points.

If reported as a paid settlement, the item will remain on the credit report for 7½ years from the date of the first late pay that led to the paid settlement. See Chapter 14 under "When Does the 7-Year Reporting Period Start."

How Long Before You Can Buy Another Home After A Short Sale?

The current guidelines from Fannie Mae & Freddie Mac state that the waiting period for a Short Sale is 2 years from the date the Short Sale proceeding is completed

There is no exception for extenuating circumstances.

The Mortgage Forgiveness Debt Relief Act Of 2007

When the lender decides to forgive all or a portion of the debt and accept less, the forgiven amount is considered as income for the borrower; leaving it open to be taxed. However, The Mortgage Forgiveness Debt Relief Act of 2007 contains amendments to remove such tax liability, allowing the borrower and lender to work together to find a solution beneficial to both parties. [3]

Bankruptcy Mortgage Relief

Currently, bankruptcy offers very limited protection to a homeowner who is upside down with his or her payments. The borrower can file a Chapter 7 which, depending on the state bankruptcy law, will most likely require him or her to surrender the property to the bankruptcy court, or file a Chapter 13 debt repayment plan to spread out prior delinquent payments over a number of months or years in the future. However, no bankruptcy proceeding can modify the terms of an existing home loan on a principal residence. Legislation is being proposed to Congress that would allow bankruptcy judges to modify the terms of an existing mortgage loan. I would not hold my breath. It could take years to make further substantial changes to the bankruptcy laws.

How Long Before You Can Buy Another Home After Bankruptcy?

The current guidelines from Fannie Mae & Freddie Mac state the waiting period for a Chapter 7 Bankruptcy is 4 years from either the dismissal or discharge date. The exception for extenuating circumstances is 2 years.

The current guidelines state that the waiting period for a Chapter 13 Bankruptcy is 2 years from either the dismissal or discharge date. There are no exceptions for extenuating circumstances.

In the case of multiple bankruptcies, the current guidelines state that the waiting period is 5 years from the most recent discharge or dismissal date. The exception for extenuating circumstances is 3 years from the most recent discharge or dismissal date.

The exception for extenuating circumstances in the case of multiple bankruptcies is a 3-year waiting period from the most recent discharge or dismissal date.

CREDIT TIP

If you are facing a foreclosure, short sale or bankruptcy due to circumstances of losing a job, a medical crisis, the subprime mortgage crisis fallout, I suggest that you fully document your experience —starting now. It's not recommended to wait until later, because, if you decide to apply for a loan in two years based on an extenuating circumstance claim, the details and emotional energy of what you are going through will be more difficult to document and prove down the road.

There Is Good News!

- **Aging Out**: In all instances above where I reference how many points will be lost in each scenario, it is important to understand that over time all derogatory accounts age out. This means that the older the account, the less it will hurt your credit scores.

- **7-Year Reporting Period:** The law states that derogatory items "can be" reported for 7-10 years. It doesn't state that they "MUST BE." My experience proves over and over again that there is no need to wait out the 7 years. You don't have to. You can start seeking early removal of the item by disputing to the credit bureaus that are reporting it. In many instances, the item will be deleted after 3-4 years.

- **You can start recovering and rebuilding immediately**. This book provides dozens of tips and tools to help you rebuild credit. For the most up-to-date information for recovering in the current credit market, please visit my website, http://www.lindaferrari.com.

Which Is The Best Choice To Protect Credit Scores?

Each of the scenarios I have presented in this chapter has a specific impact on credit scores, but it's important that each individual understands that this is a very personal decision. A borrower must weigh the impact such a critical decision will have on family, employment, and future financial stability.

But above all, consumers should not be afraid to ask questions and find out what options are available. Many consumers mistakenly assume that

222

there are specific laws and policies set in place that govern the actions of lenders, creditors, and credit bureaus. However, in many instances they are in the grey as much as the consumer. So homeowners in trouble should not feel intimated by them. If a plan sounds logical then the borrower should do the research, lay out the plan, and present it to the lender. With so many Americans in trouble, this is a time when real solutions are necessary to our economy. By creating solutions, there is a chance we can bring about changes in legislation that can help millions of consumers.

THE REAL DEAL

Over many years in the credit business I've seen much devastation to credit scores, the result of economic crisis. I have never witnessed such a dramatic impact across a wide cross-section of people as with the current mortgage debacle. It is trying the hearts, minds, and financial futures of literally millions of individuals. On a daily basis, I suffer heartbreak as I speak with countless individuals who have abandoned their last hope of salvaging their home ownership and now fight to save their credit. They are strong, and they will overcome this struggle because they are proactive; they are wise, and they know that they can take steps to mitigate the damage and recover to come back stronger than ever.

My advice to any homeowner on the verge of foreclosure is, first and foremost, find out what options are available. Do the research. Consult the experts. Gather as much information as possible, and weigh the pros and cons. What may seem to be the best answer right now may also have a serious impact for many years to come, so make an educated decision.

The great news is that whatever decision you make, whatever fate falls upon your credit scores right now, you can start improving your situation immediately.

[1]https://www.efanniemae.com/sf/guides/ssg/relatedsellinginfo/pdf/0816faqs.pdf
[2] https://www.efanniemae.com/sf/guides/ssg/annltrs/pdf/2008/0816.pdf
[3]http://www.irs.gov/irs/article/0,,id=179073,00.html

CHAPTER 20

Divorce & Credit
He Said – She Said
What About What
The Judge Said?

One out of every two marriages ends in divorce; a daunting statistic that brings with it an abundance of emotional and financial upheaval. This statistic suggests an urgent need for you to be aware of how to protect your credit standing in the face of a major life change that will significantly impact your financial situation.

While a divorce may be easy to obtain and in short order, the financial and credit issues that emanate from the dissolution can linger for years. Confusion or disagreement about who will pay what bills and who uses specific credit cards can wreak havoc on your credit scores. Late pays, no pays, and insufficient funds can quickly cause the very best credit scores to plummet. But it doesn't have to be that way. By proactively taking just a few simple steps, even when starting over you can be sure that you do everything in your power to do so with your good credit intact.

Your Divorce Decree Has No Pull

Unlike bankruptcy, when you divorce, creditors are not a party to a divorce decree; meaning that if both spouses signed the original application for credit, then both spouses are responsible until the debt is paid in full, no matter what the court document orders. This is unfair, I agree. But where it really becomes unfair is:

1. When one spouse files for bankruptcy and includes the joint debts in the filing. The ex-spouse who isn't a party to the bankruptcy is not protected and can still be held responsible for the debts.

2. When one of the ex-spouses dies, once again the remaining spouse is held liable for the debt.

Unfortunately, when it comes to these two instances, options are limited except for hiring legal help. However, there is a way to protect your credit rating during and after a divorce and that's by initiating a proactive action plan immediately.

Be Proactive – Gather Information

As soon as there is a thought that divorce or legal separation may be an option:

1. **Get Copies Of Your Credit Reports.** Request copies of your credit report from each of the three major credit bureaus, Equifax, Experian and TransUnion so you will have full insight into your current situation.

2. **Get All Of Your Information Into One Place.** Make a list of all OPEN accounts and accounts with balances. Then create a spreadsheet with columns for the following information:

    a) Creditor Name

    b) Creditor Contact Number (if it's not listed on the credit report, you can find the customer service number on the back of your statement, or you can always find it on the internet)

    c) Account Number (sometimes credit reports do not list the full account number, so you may have to dig up your paperwork)

    d) Type of Account (i.e. auto loan, mortgage, credit card)

    e) Current status of the account (i.e., current, past due, collection, etc.)

    f) Total amount due

g)   Monthly Payment Amount

h)   Ownership of Account (i.e. Joint/Individual/ Authorized Signer)

Acting On The Information

Once you've assembled your information in one place, you can determine how best to handle the accounts. You'll be dealing with two types of accounts: secured and unsecured. Each is handled very differently during a divorce. As discussed in previous chapters, secured accounts are all accounts with an asset attached to them, i.e., a mortgage or a car loan. Unsecured accounts are debts with no assets backing them up, i.e. credit card accounts.

1.   **Unsecured Accounts—Your Options**

   •   **Eliminate Obligations Where You Can.** A credit card or a statement with your name on it does not make you a joint owner of the account. Unless the account was originally opened with an application *signed by you*, you may only be an authorized signer and can request to have the item removed from your credit reports and your name removed from the account immediately. In contrast, if your spouse is on the account as an authorized signer you will want to have his or her name removed to avoid any future charges.

   CREDIT TIP

   NEVER ASSUME joint ownership of an account. Call every creditor to confirm whether or not you are joint owner or an authorized user. In a divorce, this could be a life-saver when it comes to your credit.

   •   **Close Joint Accounts.** If there's no balance, call the creditor and close the account immediately. This is one of the few times that you should close credit card accounts.

   •   **Freeze Any Future Charges.** If there's a balance that cannot be paid off right away, call the creditor and request that the account be frozen from future charges. This will allow you to pay off the balance over time without making you vulnerable to more debt. Such an action will stop both spouses from using the account; so before you take that course of action, it's important that you make certain you have another credit card in your own name.

- **Transfer Balances To Responsible Party's Individual Card.** Request that the court ordered responsible spouse transfer the remaining balances from a joint card to another credit card in his or her name only. Then close the joint account immediately.

WORD OF CAUTION

REMEMBER: Closed credit card accounts with balances are a negative line item on your credit reports and bring down your scores. If possible, make sure that the balance has been paid before closing the accounts.

2. **Secured Accounts—Your Options**

- **Sell It.** This is the safest and best option. You sell the asset, pay off the loan in full, wipe the slate clean and move on.

- **Refi It.** If the spouse responsible for paying the mortgage can qualify for a refinance in his or her own name, or has a family member who can assist with the loan, you can have the spouse buy you out completely; then you can walk away without any future obligation and have your name removed from the account.

- **Be Careful.** The least desirable option is to keep your name on the loan with certain terms and conditions. This option leaves your credit vulnerable to the responsible spouse's actions going forward. A late payment or a default on the loan will damage your credit.

Tips To Help Keep Your Credit In Tact During A Divorce

1. **Make Sure The Bills Get Paid, No Matter What the Judge Says.** Regardless of what the divorce decree stipulates, it does not override your account agreements with your creditors. Both spouses are liable and responsible for joint debt regardless of whom the judge

orders to pay the bill. If the bills are not paid and an account defaults, both spouses can be sued and both spouses can have their wages garnished. Most late pays occur during the divorce negotiations phase. Don't allow this to happen. One 30-day late can drop your credit scores by 80 points, and it takes months to gain those points back.

2. **Protect Yourself In Joint Account Situations.** The best way to handle joint accounts is to eliminate those accounts whenever possible. Because joint accounts are approved using the information from both spouses' credit reports, a creditor will not remove one spouse's name from an account regardless of whether court documents declare a specific spouse responsible for payment.

3. **If You Decide To Leave Your Name On A Secured Loan Account, Be Sure Your Name Remains On The Title.** Once your name is removed from the title, you no longer own the asset. This means that if the responsible spouse defaults on the loan and you have to pay it to save your credit scores, you'll be paying for something that you no longer own.

4. **Make sure to document and follow-up.** If you've had accounts paid and closed during the divorce proceedings, make sure your credit report reflects those changes. Follow-up on every item that relates to your credit and continue to do so until you have proof that every item is correctly stated or removed from the report. It can take many months to complete this process. Don't quit until you're certain that all loose ends are wrapped up.

5. **FINALLY,** putting the action plan to work as early in the divorce process as possible will ensure that your credit will be protected to the greatest extent possible. Decisive, quick action will *empower you to move forward.*

Real Life Success Story: Carol — My Ex Keeps Applying For Credit – IN MY NAME!

I am bringing this true story to your attention because I've seen it happen many times.

Carol was in the middle of a divorce. She was working with a mediation company to settle financial issues, such as child support, alimony, and the division of property. The mediator suggested that Carol consider re-financing the family home into her name alone to relieve her ex-spouse of the mortgage payment. When Carol had her credit pulled, she found that her soon-to-be ex had opened three credit card accounts in her name, two of them had been maxed out and one was in delinquent status. As a result, there was NO WAY she would be able to refinance her home.

Carol called the creditors and explained that she did not open the accounts. Despite her efforts, she was continuously told that the records showed otherwise. Obviously her ex had signed her name to the accounts, but this seemed to make no difference to the creditors who continued to hold Carol responsible. Now this is when most consumers give in; they pay the debts, suffer the credit hit because they are led to believe they can't prevail or that the path to victory is too difficult.

Carol came to me to find out what her options were. After reviewing her case, it was easy for me to give her some suggestions. This is what we did:

1. Carol called all three credit grantors and asked for copies of the fraudulent applications and transaction records. Both federal and California law give you the right to obtain these documents under FCRA § 609(e), and California Penal Code 530.8. We also followed up our phone request with a certified written request.

2. We called two of Carol's real creditors, and her bank, and had them fax us a copy of her signed agreements and bank signature cards to validate her own signature.

3. We filled out an Identity Theft Report on the Federal Trade Commission Identity Theft Site at http://www.ftc.gov.

4. Once we received the items in 1. and 2. above, we composed a formal "request for removal" letter to each creditor that was reporting the fraudulent accounts. We included the following:

   a) Her story and claim of Identity Theft.

   b) Copies of the fraudulent documents in 1. (above) and completed Affidavit forms that we received from each of the creditors reporting the fraudulent accounts.

    c) Copies of the true signature documents described in 2. (above) to prove the difference in signatures.

    d) A copy of the Identity Theft Report.

The letter also referenced the Fair and Accurate Credit Transaction Act, and the Fair Credit Reporting Act, and included a couple of news stories on successful lawsuits won by identity theft victims against creditors and credit bureaus that refused to update consumer files as required by law after complaints of identity theft.

Within two months, all three credit bureaus had removed the derogatory and fraudulent accounts from Carol's credit reports and her scores shot back up to the mid-700s. It was a very good day for Carol. And to think she almost gave up and took the heat. There are ALWAYS options. There are always ways to improve a bad credit situation.

THE REAL DEAL

Divorce can be very tough emotionally and financially. Acting proactively about your credit can minimize the fallout. Though it may seem challenging at first, you will soon find that putting the above recommendations into action is easily done once you get started. You will also put behind you a crucial first step toward moving on with your life and establishing your financial independence.

CHAPTER 21

Identity Theft

Imagine what it would be like to wake up one morning to find bills for credit cards you've never applied for, phone bills under your name that don't belong to you, or getting a threatening call from a collector wanting payment for a car you didn't buy. You would probably be confused and frustrated at first. Then that confusion would turn to anger and fear once you realize that your credit—and your good name—have been severely damaged. What would you do? How would you undo it? How much money has already been spent in your name? How did this happen? How many "you's" are there out there in the world applying for jobs, credit, and a driver's license in your name?

Unfortunately, this scenario is exactly what thousands of people experience every day. It is identity theft, and it is growing in the U.S. at an alarming rate. Now more than ever, a person's identity has become his or her most valuable asset. Protecting that asset is paramount not only for your safety but also for your ability to acquire credit. There are numerous villains out there preying on innocent victims who simply do not know how to protect their identities from being stolen.

True Story — Utility Company Fraud

A client of mine, Connor, owns three successful businesses. In February, 2008, he was in the midst of remodeling one of his locations when his assistant received a phone call from the utility company allegedly to inform him that the electricity bill had not been paid on the facility that was being remodeled and that it was scheduled to be turned off at 5:00 p.m. that day. Obviously this was a big potential problem for my client.

Connor's assistant called him immediately from a second line and told him what was going on. Connor gave her his credit card information, instructing her to get the situation straightened out right away. The individual representing the electric company advised Connor's assistant that the card was declined. Flustered, Connor gave his assistant another credit card number. The representative came back stating that this card, too, had been declined. At this point, Connor knew that something was wrong, and his assumption was right.

The woman on the other line was actually an inmate calling from prison. She had already successfully racked up thousands of dollars in charges on Connor's cards by the time Connor hung up the phone.

The nature of identity theft is changing rapidly, with thieves becoming more and more clever at obtaining information. They'll break into a car not for a fancy stereo, but for a bank statement carelessly left in the back seat. They'll dig through your trash for tossed out credit card applications. They'll even ask point blank for the information and unknowing victims, not realizing the danger, will simply give them what they want.

The Facts About Identity Theft

Identity theft can be prevented! I cannot stress enough how important it is for you to protect your information. Your personal identity should be safeguarded just as you would protect your family and your home. Material possessions can be insured and replaced. Identities are one of a kind and, although the damage can be repaired, it is much easier to prevent the situation from happening.

Learning the facts about identity theft will prevent you from falling victim. Following are a handful of statistics taken from http://www.privacyrights.org/ar/idtheftsurveys.htm, the official website of Privacy Rights Clearinghouse, a non-profit consumer rights organization:

- Identity theft is now the fastest growing crime in America.

- Per the Federal Trade Commission and Consumer Federation of America, approximately 9-10 million consumers become victims of identity theft every year.

- This crime costs consumers approximately $5 billion a year and banks and institutions more than $50 billion annually to cover the total amounts stolen.

- Online transactions are the least used method by ID thieves, yet the method consumers fear most.

- It used to be that consumers were only responsible for paying $50 toward fraudulent charges made to their credit cards, but creditors have changed their contracts. In many cases, if you do not notify your creditors within a 60-day period that the charges do not belong to you, you could be personally responsible for some of those charges in full. This is why it is so important to check your statements and credit reports as often as possible.

- It is estimated that 5% of the annual 10 million identity theft victims are children who are under the age of 18.

True Story – My Daughter Was A Victim

When I heard these statistics, I was stunned. I immediately called one of the credit bureaus and asked them to look up my daughter's social security number to see if she had a credit file established. When they asked me how old she was, I told them she was 14. At that point, they basically told me not to worry because the chances were very slim that she would be a victim of identity theft. When I pursued and insisted on speaking to management, stating that I was concerned and wanted someone to look up her social security number, I finally got my way; and guess what—she did have a file. Someone had applied for credit using her social security number, but was unsuccessful.

CREDIT TIP

This is incredibly important! *Don't just settle for a pat answer.* When it comes to the credit bureaus, you have to dig deeper. Despite what they say to make you go away, you have to be insistent in your requests. It's your financial future, and your children's future. You have a right to protect it, and that begins with you asserting your right to know.

How Identities Are Stolen

Despite your best efforts to manage the flow of your personal information or to keep it to yourself, getting into the mind of a criminal is a tough thing to do. Trying to figure out the many methods a criminal knows to steal from us will always leave them in the driver's seat. Identity thieves know a million and one ways to steal your personal information. Here are some recent data breaches that show just how pervasive this crime has become.

Data Breach Facts

Per Privacy Rights Clearinghouse (PRC)—a non-profit consumer rights organization, roughly 230,441,730 data records containing information such as social security numbers, credit card account numbers, loan account information and other personal information—has been compromised in the United States since January of 2005 [1]. The top five data breaches listed in PRC's most recent report, *Chronology of Data Breaches*, are as follows:

1. Cardsystems had 40 million credit card numbers stolen from its database by computer hackers.

2. CitiFinancial lost 3.9 million financial records.

3. iBill had more than 17 million data records stolen by an insider.

4. An employee of the US Department of Veteran's Affairs had 28.6 million data records belonging to American Veterans stolen from their home.

5. Federal Trade Commission settled a data breach complaint— in which data breaches have affected more than 100 million accounts—against TJX (which owns TJ Maxx, Marshalls, Winners, HomeSense, AJWright, TKMaxx, and other retail stores located throughout the United States, United Kingdom, Canada and Ireland) and Reed Elsevier (subsidiary of LexisNexis)

I advise you to visit http://www.privacyrights.org/ar/ChronDataBreaches.htm and read the important documents there. It is tremendously important that every consumer understand the extent to which identity theft invades and impacts our lives. You need to beware of the fact that the odds are decidedly against consumers as a whole if our major creditors continue to lose our information to identity thieves.

Other Ways Identities Are Stolen

- Stealing personal information from a wallet or purse. Lost or stolen wallets and purses are still a number one method of identity theft.

- Going through mail or trash looking for items like bank statements, credit card statements, and pre-approved credit card offers.

- Redirecting mail by submitting a change of address form to the post office.

- Acquiring credit reports by pretending to be a potential landlord, or employer.

- Pretending to be a creditor calling on the phone to update account information.

- Getting information from employment records.

- Phishing scams on the internet (posing as a creditor or bank asking to update personal information in their files.)

- Computer viruses sent to your computer through emails, or pop-up banners. Once clicked, these viruses rush through your computer system looking for personal identification information, account numbers and passwords.

- Door to door salesman. Yes, believe it or not, people are still going door to door, and when you hand over that check for the most up-dated version of your encyclopedia set there's a good chance they will empty out your bank account.

Medical Identity Theft Is On The Rise

Believe it or not, identity thieves are people. When these thieves suffer an illness or injury, they go to the emergency room for treatment the same as we do. The difference between us and them? They don't give *their* information, they give other people's information—maybe even yours. The way you find this out is you start receiving medical bills, even threatening notices from collection agencies.

It's important for you to know that although you are not liable for the bill, unless you handle the situation immediately (using some of the collection or identity theft strategies outlined throughout this book to stop the reporting before it happens), you risk the unpaid items being reported on your credit reports. The key is to NOT ignore one of these bills, because avoidance will undoubtedly wreak havoc on your credit scores.

Identity Theft And The Deceased

Another astonishing fact about identity theft is that even families of deceased individuals are vulnerable. Identity thieves obtain information about deceased individuals by watching the obituaries, stealing death certificates, and acquiring information from websites that offer the Social Security Index files.

Here are some tips to help you make sure that you are not burdened by further difficulty in managing your way through the death of a loved one:

1. Immediately contact the three credit bureaus in writing and request that a "deceased" alert be placed on the credit report. Each credit bureau has specific guidelines to follow, so it is important that you call each credit bureau to ask what those guidelines are. Here are the contact numbers:

   • Equifax: (800) 685-1111

   • Experian: (888) 397-3742

   • TransUnion: (800) 916-8800

   Be sure to send each letter by certified mail. Include a copy of the death certificate and request a copy of the deceased credit report so that you can also check to make sure that identity theft hasn't already taken place.

2. Immediately notify all credit card companies, mortgage companies, banks, and, if applicable, collection agencies, of the death. They may also require that you use a specific procedure. At this time, the surviving spouse or executor will need to discuss all outstanding debts and how they will be dealt with at that time.

3. If you find that the deceased has already incurred identity theft, follow the specific guidelines that I have outlined later in this chapter.

238

4. Notify all parties first by telephone and then immediately in writing. All correspondence should be sent via certified mail. From day one, keep copies of all correspondence.

How To Prevent Identity Theft

1. Opt Out of receiving pre-approved credit card offers in the mail. Here's the phone number 1(888)5-OPTOUT, 1(888)567-8688.

2. Check credit reports regularly to make sure that the information being reported is accurate.

3. Get a cross-cut paper shredder and shred every document a person could use to steal an identity, including credit card solicitations, bank solicitations, bank statements, etc.

4. Never give out credit card numbers, social security numbers or other personal information to someone over the phone or in an email requesting that type of information.

> **CREDIT TIP**
>
> If someone calls or emails you asking you to verify information on an account, hang up the phone and call their creditor back at the telephone number on your statement to verify the request.

5. Always keep your computer's anti-spy, or anti-theft software updated with the most recent version.

6. Check bank statements every month and make sure they are correct.

7. Sign up for a credit watch program that will send an alert whenever there is activity on the credit report. For a list of companies that I send my clients to, visit my website at http://www.lindaferrari.com.

8. Make a copy of everything in your wallet and keep it somewhere safe so that you have immediate access to telephone numbers should you become a victim.

CREDIT TIP

If you live in an area conducive to severe weather conditions (such as hurricanes, floods, tornadoes,) I recommend that you send your credit information to a family member or trusted individual located in another area. Or, if you are confident that your safety deposit box would be safe through weather conditions, keep this information there.

9. Only process online credit card transactions if the site has a secured icon on it which is usually a lock, or if the URL address changes from HTTP to HTTPS. The S is for secured.

10. Find out if your state has instituted a Security Freeze law to protect people who consider themselves at risk for any reason. (This includes vulnerability for those filing for divorce!)

What To Do If You Become A Victim Of Identity Theft

If you are a victim of identity theft, take the following four steps as soon as possible, and keep a record with the details of your conversations and copies of all correspondence.

1. **Place a fraud alert on your credit reports, and review your credit reports.**

   Fraud alerts can help prevent an identity thief from opening any more accounts in your name. Contact the toll-free fraud number of any of the three credit bureaus below to place a fraud alert on your credit report. You only need to contact one of the three companies to place an alert. The company you call is required to contact the other two, which will place an alert on their versions of your report, too. If you do not receive a confirmation from a company, you should contact that company directly to place a fraud alert.

   • **Equifax:** 1-800-525-6285; http://www.equifax.com; P.O. Box 740241, Atlanta, GA 30374-0241

   • **Experian:** 1-888-EXPERIAN (397-3742); http://www.experian.com; P.O. Box 9532, Allen, TX 75013

• **TransUnion:** 1-800-680-7289; http://www.transunion.
com; Fraud Victim Assistance Division, P.O. Box 6790,
Fullerton, CA 92834-6790

Once you place the fraud alert in your file, you're entitled to order
one free copy of your credit report from each of the three consumer
reporting companies. Once you get your credit reports, review them
carefully. Look for inquiries from companies you haven't contacted,
accounts you didn't open, and debts on your accounts that you can't
explain. Check that information such as your social security number,
addresses, name or initials, and employers are correct. If you find
fraudulent or inaccurate information, follow the steps below to have
the fraudulent information removed from your credit report.

2. **Close the accounts that you know, or believe, have been tam-
pered with or opened fraudulently.**

Call and speak with someone in the security or fraud department
of each company. Follow up in writing, and include copies (NOT
originals) of supporting documents. It's important to notify credit
card companies and banks in writing. Send your letters by certified
mail, return receipt requested, so that you can document what the
company received and when. Keep a file of your correspondence
and enclosures.

When the creditor assigns a new account number, use new Personal
Identification Numbers (PINs) and passwords. Avoid using easily
available information like your mother's maiden name, your birth
date, the last four digits of your Social Security number or your
phone number, or a series of consecutive numbers.

Also, when your creditor assigns a new account number in the instance of a lost credit card, make sure that they place a fraud alert
on the old account number. I have seen many identity theft charges
made through online telephone orders on old account numbers that
were supposed to have been cancelled.

If the identity thief has made charges or debits on your accounts, or
has fraudulently opened accounts, ask the company for the forms to
dispute those transactions:

- For charges and debits on existing accounts, ask the representative to send you the company's fraud dispute forms. If the company doesn't have special forms, use the sample letter from the ftc.gov site at http://www.ftc.gov/bcp/edu/microsites/idtheft/downloads/dispute-letter-for-exisiting-accounts.doc to dispute the fraudulent charges or debits. In either case, write to the company at the address given for billing inquiries, NOT to the address for sending your payments.

- If you want to file a dispute directly with the company, and do not want to file a report with the police, ask if the company accepts the FTC's ID Theft Affidavit. You will find this form on the Federal Trade Commission's Identity Theft site at http://www.ftc.gov/bcp/edu/microsites/idtheft/index.html. If it does not, ask the representative to send you the company's fraud dispute forms.

- Filing a report with the police and then providing the company with an Identity Theft Report will give you greater protection. For example, if the company has already reported these unauthorized accounts or debits on your credit report, an Identity Theft Report will require them to stop reporting that fraudulent information. In your cover letter, explain to the company the rights you have by using the Identity Theft Report. More information about getting and using an Identity Theft Report can be found at http://www.ftc.gov.

- Once you have resolved your identity theft dispute with the company, ask for a letter stating that the company has closed the disputed accounts and has discharged the fraudulent debts. This letter is your best proof if errors relating to this account reappear on your credit report or if you are contacted again about the fraudulent debt.

3. **File a complaint with the Federal Trade Commission.**

You can file a complaint online with the FTC at http://www.ftc.gov/bcp/edu/microsites/idtheft/index.html; or call the FTC's Identity Theft Hotline, toll-free: 1-877-ID-THEFT (438-4338); or write Identity Theft Clearinghouse, Federal Trade Commission, 600 Pennsylvania Avenue, NW, Washington, DC 20580. If you have any additional information or problems, be sure to call the Hotline to update your complaint.

By sharing your identity theft complaint with the FTC, you will provide important information that can help law enforcement officials across the nation track down and stop identity thieves. The FTC can refer victims' complaints to other government agencies and companies for further action, as well as to investigate companies for violations of laws the agency enforces.

Additionally, you can provide a printed copy of your online Complaint form to the police to incorporate into their police report. The printed FTC ID Theft Complaint, in conjunction with the police report, can constitute an Identity Theft Report and entitle you to certain protections. This Identity Theft Report can be used to: 1) permanently block fraudulent information from appearing on your credit report; 2) ensure that debts do not reappear on your credit report; 3) prevent a company from continuing to collect debts that result from identity theft; and 4) place an extended fraud alert on your credit report.

4.   **File a report with your local police or the police in the community where the identity theft took place.**

Call your local police department and tell them that you want to file a report about your identity theft. Ask them if you can file the report in person. If you cannot, ask if you can file a report over the internet or telephone.

If the police are reluctant to take your report, you have three options: 1) You can ask to file a "Miscellaneous Incident" report; 2) Try another jurisdiction, like your state police; or 3) Give them a copy of the FTC's Law Enforcement Letter that you can download from   http://www.ftc.gov/bcp/edu/microsites/idtheft/index.html. You can also check with your state Attorney General's office to find out if state law requires the police to take reports for identity theft. If so, you can use that information to force the issue.

When you go to your local police department to file your report, bring a printed copy of your FTC ID Theft Complaint form described above in 3. and a cover letter with any supporting documentation.

Ask the officer to attach or incorporate the ID Theft Complaint into their police report. Tell them that you need a copy of the Identity Theft Report (the police report with your ID Theft Complaint attached or incorporated) to dispute the fraudulent accounts and debts created by the identity thief. (In some jurisdictions the officer will not be able to give you a copy of the official police report, but should be able to sign your Complaint and write the police report number in the "Law Enforcement Report" section.)

Tips On How To Recover Your Credit After Identity Theft

Recovering from Identity Theft can be extremely difficult. However, if you follow the guidelines outlined above from the Federal Trade Commission, and use some of the following tips, you will be able to move forward from a devastating situation with more ease. The good news is that legislators are paying attention to this crime more than ever before, as evidenced by the passing of the Fair and Accurate Credit Transaction Act (FACTA). FACTA was specifically designed to help protect consumers against Identity Theft. In Chapter 13, you can review a summary of consumer protections under FACTA.

Here are some more tips to help consumers recover from Identity Theft:

- Do everything that you can to avoid identity theft by following the recommendations laid out in this chapter.

- File the Federal Trade Commission's recommended documentation immediately. Don't wait.

- Send all correspondence via certified mail to prove delivery. You will need proof of delivery should a creditor or credit bureau resist removal of an item of identity theft from your credit reports.

- Keep logs of everything.

- Visit FTC's Identity Theft Website: Fighting Back Against Identity

Theft at http://www.ftc.gov/bcp/edu/microsites/idtheft/index.html.

*   IMPORTANT — Check your credit reports every 2-3 months for at least one year after the identity theft issue is resolved.

*   Continue to maintain and manage all of your open accounts. Do not stop paying because of identity theft issues on other accounts.

*   You may want to check your criminal history report just to be safe. You can do so at the Federal Bureau of Investigation's web site at http://www.fbi.gov/hq/cjisd/fprequest.htm.

THE REAL DEAL

Identity theft can make you feel violated. Undoing the damage to your credit scores and your life can be frustrating, long and unsettling, not to mention the invasive feeling that someone has been posing as you. The best defense against identity theft is to reduce your vulnerability to it. Be PROACTIVE and join a credit watch program so that you can check your credit reports every 3-4 months. Remember, as consumers, it is ultimately up to us to protect our greatest asset. Being aware and following the guidelines above can go a long way to keep your personal identity safe, private, and secure.

A final note regarding Identity Theft: It's important to know that this area of credit is ever evolving, and new scams are always cropping up. For this reason, it's very important to stay on top of the latest scams. You can find links to ID Theft sites that will make you aware of the most current scams by visiting my website at http://www.lindaferrari.com.

[1] http://www.privacyrights.org/ar/ChronDataBreaches.htm#2007

CHAPTER 22

Taking Action

Regardless of where you are with your credit scores and management, there are specific steps you can take to further improve a good situation and/or make a bad situation better. Taking action doesn't just apply to people who have serious credit challenges. According to Fair Isaac & Co., the top credit score is 850, however, *too many consumers settle for less*—sometimes far less. Even if you have a 720 credit score, you can and should take action to improve those scores NOW. This is important because you are just a handful of points away from excellent credit to the upside, and mediocre credit to the downside.

By coming so far in this book, you know you can prevail by using the tips set forth in each chapter. Your best tool is the knowledge you have gained. *Trust it and use it.*

The most important advice I can give you is that you cannot go halfway with this plan. Your best and longest lasting results will come to you if you commit to a credit improvement and lifetime maintenance plan, and follow through on that commitment. Each step you take when dealing with credit bureaus and creditors is time sensitive—based on the calendar. If you drop the ball, you give them the upper hand.

The credit bureaus, collection agencies, and creditors count on you to get bored, get busy, or get frustrated and give up. Knowing this, they'll do everything they can to wear you down. They'll turn a simple dispute to correct a name spelling into a three-month battle, and unfortunately, other than to follow-up diligently and stick to the plan, there's nothing you can do about it. But, when you know you are right, DO NOT BACK DOWN. For your best success, you need to prioritize your battles. Don't overwhelm yourself.

Just handling one issue at a time will move you in a positive direction with your credit scores and empower you.

The alternative is to do nothing, and I trust by now you realize just how much doing nothing will cost you in the long-run. In fact, sometimes just the failure to handle certain issues can be construed as validation that the derogatory is true and accurate, even when it is not.

If you've determined that you can and should take action to improve your credit situation, you have everything you need right here—in the pages of this book—to begin right now. If, on the other hand, you've decided that you need to take action but simply don't have the time or inclination, don't be unfazed. I would strongly advise you to hire a professional to help you get going. See Chapter 3 for tips on hiring a reputable company. Don't just leave it alone, set it aside, or ignore it. You can take it on, and all action you take will serve you well—and sooner than you think.

Linda's 10-Step TAP (*Take Action Plan*)

Congratulations! So far, by reading this book you have developed an understanding of the importance of good credit, the pitfalls of poor credit, and how you can solve so many of the devastating credit issues that prevent consumers from living out their financial dreams. Now, you are fully prepared to embark on my signature TAP, the Take Action Plan that provides step-by-step instructions for moving ahead with better credit management for life.

As a caution for reading this chapter: If, as you read through this section, you feel as if you are not absorbing all of the information, DON'T WORRY. I encourage you to just keep reading through, and then read the chapter or the section again to get more clarity. This information will all sink in. Just be patient and realize that you are working on making a permanent change in your life and that staying the course will pay off big. Remember, saving your credit can save your life.

Here are the steps, plain and simple:

1. Set Your Score Goal

2. Get Your Credit Reports

3. Read Your Credit Reports

4. Make Your TAP Checklist

5. Decide & Act: Dispute, Negotiate or Wait

6. Get Your Mix In Check

7. Manage Your Debt Strategically

8. Disputing Do's & Don'ts

9. What If You Don't Have Credit?

10. Commit to a Maintenance Plan

Step 1: Set Your Score Goal

The first step toward the success of any plan is to define your goals. Goals can be short term, long term, reasons, or specific items. Here are some examples of why consumers may want to start taking action on improving their credit scores NOW:

1. To make the most of your current credit rating.

2. To purchase a new home, auto, or send your kids to college.

3. To refinance your existing home or auto loan.

4. To lower interest rates on all of your accounts so that you can save more money for retirement.

5. To be in a position of financial freedom at all times. Being able to walk into a mortgage lender, auto lender, or bank and not ever having to worry about being denied credit. I call this *Credit Ability.*

These are great reasons, but they all have one thing in common; they all require strong credit scores. Having reasons is good start. Yet in my experience—coaching and motivating thousands of individuals to commit to a take action credit score improvement plan—I have found that setting your ultimate score goal is what creates the desire to succeed. I make sure that my clients have all of the information they need to be realistic in setting their goal score, and then, once they plant that number in their mind, and they have access to the tools to succeed, there is usually no stopping their progress. Every time their scores go up, even just a few points, it's exhilarating because they know that every point brings them closer to something that will change not only their life for the better, but that of their family, present or future.

If you have read this book in its entirety, then you have access to the tools and information you need to set your minimum score goal right now. It should be nothing less than a 750.

Write it down in places where you look everyday. Your calendar, your notebook, a note on your monitor, a note on your refrigerator. To stay motivated, positive reinforcement is essential.

Be realistic about timing. If you have credit challenges such as collections, charge-offs and public records, then allow at least 6-12 months to start seeing substantial improvement in your credit scores. However, if your credit challenges are basic, which includes general clean-up, credit card balance issues, or not enough credit, then you need at least 3-6 months.

Either way, remember that every feat, small or large, deserves appreciation. One point can save you thousands of dollars; and one point can make the difference of whether or not you have access to funds to send your kids to college. Set your goal score TODAY!

Step 2: Get Your Credit Reports

Today, you have access to your credit information all day and every day. This is wonderful news. Consumers now have the opportunity to quickly correct and maintain credit reports. It is mission critical for consumers to seize that advantage by assuming responsibility. Lenders, employers, and vendors judge us based on our credit reports, and they know that we are capable of doing so. The days of excuses are in the rearview mirror.

You can get started by acquiring a copy of your credit report from each of the three major bureaus. It's important to get reports from each of the three—not just one. The bureaus do not share data, so you need to get a full accounting of everything that is being reported.

You options are as follows:

1. **Reports from the credit bureaus.** As discussed in Chapter 5, the reports that you receive directly from the three credit bureaus are easy to read. More importantly, going straight to the source of the

data will ensure that your action plan begins with the most complete information being reported about you. This includes your credit accounts, your credit history, and your personal and demographic information. My advice is to cut to the chase, and go direct.

You can order your credit report and score from each credit bureau on line, through the mail, or via telephone. Here is the information you need:

- Equifax: (800) 685-1111 - http://www.equifax.com
  Cost: $15.95

- Experian: (888) 397-3742 - http://www.experian.com
  Cost: $15.00

- TransUnion: (800) 916-8800 - http://www.transunion.com
  Cost: $14.95

As strange as it seems, I have found that the bureaus change their addresses without warning. So when ready to contact the bureaus by mail, be sure to call for their current mailing information. You can also use these numbers to order your reports by phone.

WORD OF CAUTION

When you log onto each site, they will try to up sell you with many different products, including credit watch programs or 3-in-1 credit reports and scores for three times the price. Make sure that you only purchase the credit report and score from that bureau.

If you have been denied credit or insurance within the last 60 days, if you are disabled, unemployed, or on welfare, you may be entitled to a free copy of your credit report. If this is the case, send a written request to each credit bureau. In your letter, be sure to order your credit score. The cost for the score is approximately $7.95 per bureau, but I always recommend calling the bureau directly to confirm the fees.

2. **Free credit reports.** By law, each of the nationwide consumer reporting companies, Equifax, Experian, and TransUnion, must pro-

vide a free copy of your credit report, at your request, once every 12 months. To read more about this, a good source is the Federal Trade Commission's Consumer Alert that you can download at http://www.ftc.gov/bcp/edu/pubs/consumer/alerts/alt156.pdf.

You can access this program in one of three ways:

a) Go to http://www.annualcreditreport.com;

b) Call 1-877-322-8228; or

c) Complete the Annual Credit Report Request Form and mail it to: Annual Credit Report Request Service, P.O. Box 105281, Atlanta, GA 30348-5281. You can download the form with instructions at http://www.ftc.gov/bcp/edu/pubs/consumer/alerts/alt156.pdf.

WORD OF CAUTION

I understand that during financial hardship, free credit reports are very tempting; however, I must warn you that these reports are very difficult to read.

Remember, this program does not offer free credit scores. I highly recommend that if you decide to take advantage of this program that you order your scores at the same time. Again the fee is usually around $7.95 per bureau.

A Warning About "Imposter" Websites

Only http://www.annualcreditreport.com is authorized to provide the free annual credit report mandated by law. Other websites make claims for "free credit reports," "free credit scores," or "free credit monitoring," but they are not affiliated with the program, and they are likely trying to sell you something.

3. **Credit reports from an online vendor.** Not for this part of the plan! As discussed in Chapter 5, hundreds of websites offer credit reports and scores to consumers. To assemble your take action plan, I advise that you begin right away with one of the two options above. Online reports are great for maintenance, but they do not

give you the full picture of ALL data that each credit bureau is storing in your file.

Step 3: Read Your Credit Reports

Laws have made it easier for you to access your reports, but they haven't made those reports easier to understand. I have to tell you, though, credit reports have come a long way since I saw my first credit report which struck me as looking more like NASA code than my credit history. I was so intimidated by the data that I gave up trying to figure it out. So, like many other people, I put it out of my mind and avoided my credit reports. I lived in ignorant bliss—that is, until the day I was denied credit! Well, if I had any excuses, you don't. I can promise you that today's credit reports are NOT rocket science. I have personally witnessed thousands of individuals grasp an understanding of their credit reports after only one consultation with me.

There are hundreds of different credit report formats in use today. An explanation of each would not only make for a very boring read, but it would also be impossible for me to teach you in this book how to read each format. The good news is that you don't have to know how to read every format to manage your credit. Once you learn the basics, you will be able to apply your knowledge to any credit report you lay your eyes on. Hopefully, you'll take my advice and start your take action plan using the reports directly from the three credit bureaus. Here are some helpful hints on what to look for as it relates to the format of each:

- **Equifax** mixes positive and negative trade lines. This makes Equifax's report the most difficult to read. As a general rule, Equifax will list public records first, and most collections separately. However, sometimes collections are intermingled with other trade lines, so review every trade line carefully and thoroughly. Late pays are listed at the very bottom of each trade line under the section title "Account History with Status Codes." Personal identification and demographic information is on the first page, and inquiries are listed in the back of the report.

- **Experian** separates positive from negative all the time. As a general rule, Experian will list public records first, then all "Potentially Negative Items or Items For Further Review," followed by "Accounts In Good Standing." Inquiries, and personal identification and demographic information are located in the back of the report.

- **TransUnion** follows suit with Experian, by clearly separating positive from negative accounts all the time. As a general rule, TransUnion will list public records first, then all "Adverse Accounts," followed by all "Satisfactory Accounts." Personal identification and demographic information are on the first page, and inquiries are listed in the back of the report.

CREDIT TIP

When you dispute with a credit bureau, they will respond with a copy of your updated credit report. So if your action plan begins with an online version of your credit report from each credit bureau, the version that you receive in response to your dispute will be different. Don't be thrown off. The online reports give very clear instructions on how to read the data, including translation of codes, etc. The mailed version, although a different format, contains the same exact information, just laid out differently.

Step 4: Create Your TAP Checklist

In my business, I use "The Home Inspection Analogy." When you want to sell your home, you hire an inspector. They make a detailed "fix it list" of the items in need of repair. The theory is that the more items completed on this list, the more you will maximize the value of your home. It's the same with credit. Your goal is to go through your credit reports with a fine-tooth comb, make a list of the items that are negatively impacting your scores, and know that the more items you check off your list the better chance you have of maximizing your credit scores in the shortest period of time.

When most people look at their credit reports, they focus on repairing the negative items. It is critically important for you to remember that negative payment history only makes up 35% of your scores. There is another 65% of your scores that has nothing to do with negative payment history but still brings down the scores. It is essential that you make sure that all of your good credit is being reported and being reported accurately.

Before making your TAP Checklist, you will want to create a workable spreadsheet that will organize the data and action plan in a way that will give you instant indication of what action needs to be taken. You can download my 10-Step TAP Worksheet from my site at http://www.lindaferrari.com, or you can create your own. At minimum, your spreadsheet should include the following columns:

- Item Type (i.e. collection, late pay, wrong name, tax lien)

- Dispute Reason

- Account Status (open or closed)

- Original Creditor Name & Account #

- Collection Agency/Court Name and Account or Case #

- Open Date

- Date of Last Delinquency or Date Paid

- A column to list the Statute of Limitation Date

- A column to list the 7-Year Reporting Date

- Amount Due

- Limit

- Balance

- Action (Dispute, Negotiate, Wait)

- First Dispute/VOD Letter Date

- Reinvestigation Letter Date

- Formal No Response Complaint Date

- Letter of Intent to Sue Date

One of the columns in your spreadsheet will be the dispute reason. To help you get started, here's a list of 30 of the most common dispute reasons. If any of these apply to the information being reported on your credit reports, you should consider the item negative and add that item to your TAP checklist:

1. This account does not belong to me.

2. I was not 30, 60, 90 or 120 days late on this account.

3. This is a duplicate account.

4. I never authorized this account.

5. The balance on this account is incorrect.

6. There is no past due balance on this account.

7. You are not reporting a positive account on my credit report.

8. This account is closed with a $0 balance and has a positive history.

9. This account was closed by me, not the creditor.

10. You are not reporting the correct limit on my account.

11. This account was included in a bankruptcy and should have a $0 balance.

12. This account was paid.

13. The open date on this account is incorrect.

14. This account is still open.

15. I am only an authorized user on this account. Please remove it.

16. You are reporting my home equity line of credit as a revolving account.

17. I never authorized this inquiry.

18. This public record has been satisfied/released/dismissed/vacated.

19. You are listing the wrong file/released/satisfied date on this public record.

20. This account was charged off in (date). No late pays should be reported after that date.

21. The date of last activity on this account is incorrect.

22. This account never went into foreclosure/repossession.

23. The 7-year reporting period has expired on this account.

24. The statute of limitations on this account expired. You cannot report it or re-insert it.

25. You are reporting someone else's information on my credit report that has the same name that I do.

26. You are reporting the wrong social security number, birth date, spouse's name, phone number on my credit report.

27. You are reporting wrong/expired/misspelled addresses on my credit report.

28. You are reporting misspelled/wrong names on my credit report.

29. You are reporting outdated/wrong employment information on my credit report.

30. This student loan account has been deferred.

The key is to make three separate TAP spreadsheets, one for each credit bureau, and to write down *EVERYTHING* that needs attention. Then, using the knowledge you've gained from reading this book, you can decide which action should be taken—Dispute, Negotiate, or Wait.

Step 5: Decide & Act: Dispute, Negotiate, or Wait

Now it's time to take action. This means taking the steps to get the items on your list updated, corrected, or removed. Throughout this book, I have given you access to tools, tips, information and even legal references that will help you successfully dispute and negotiate with the credit bureaus and creditors; so for the purposes of this chapter, I will outline the basics. You have three choices, as follows:

Dispute

If your decision is to dispute an item, you must be ready to commit and follow through. Here are some basic tips to get you started:

1. Send a letter to the credit bureaus giving them a detailed explanation of what you are requesting. Attach copies of any supporting documentation that you have (i.e. statements proving your correct credit card limits and proof of payments). Send letters certified,

and, to avoid delay in their replies, always attach proof of social security and proof of address right from the beginning.

2. Wait 35 days (allowing 5 days for mail time.) If the bureaus do not respond within 35 days, send a formal complaint letter reminding them that per Section 611 of the Fair Credit Reporting Act they are required to respond within 30 days from the date they received your initial dispute. Also remind them that per Section 616 & 617 of the same Act they are liable for damages, including punitive, and that if necessary you will seek legal representation. Attach your original dispute letter and proof of delivery to the complaint.

3. Just because the credit bureau has determined an item "investigated" does not mean the results are accurate. If you are 100% sure that your claim is true and accurate, and the bureau responds stating that the creditor has verified the information and the item will not be removed or updated, you must request a reinvestigation under Section 611 of the Fair Credit Reporting Act. I highly recommend that you do so within 5 days of receiving the results of their investigation. You can repeat this process as many times as you want; however, after three to four attempts, I would consider moving onto the next step.

4. If the credit bureau continues to stand it's ground on not updating or correcting inaccurate items on your credit report, see Chapters 13 and 18, where I talk about suing the credit bureaus and collection agencies and WINNING! Here are a couple of additional tips:

    a) As discussed in Chapter 13, attaching copies of lawsuit verdicts that show how consumers have prevailed against the bureaus can help you convince the credit bureaus to make the necessary changes to your reports. It lets them know that you are well aware of your consumer rights.

    b) Look for other consumer stories on the web. There are tons of credit repair chat rooms in which consumers share their strategies. As you know, you don't want to take advice out of blind trust, but now that you have read this book you have a better understanding of the reasoning behind certain actions that pertain to credit improvement. Within that framework, you may find some helpful tips.

c) File a complaint with the Federal Trade Commission Consumer Response Center. You may be able to have your case added to a class action lawsuit against the bureau that is reporting the inaccurate information. You can access the FTC Complaint Wizard at http://www.ftc.gov/bcp/index.shtml, or you can mail a complaint letter to the following address:

Federal Trade Commission
Consumer Response Center
600 Pennsylvania Avenue, NW
Washington, DC 20580

Negotiate

In Chapter 15, I talk at great length about consumer debt relief options. I also talk, in Chapter 18, about negotiating collection debt for pennies on the dollar. The most important advice I can give you about negotiating is:

* Negotiate with confidence that you will win. You now have everything you need, including access to key laws and powerful tips. The reason consumers do not succeed in negotiating is because they don't have the knowledge *that you now have*. Knowledge is power, and once the collection agency or creditor realizes that you have done your research, not only will you limit their response options but they will realize immediately that you are not a pushover. The tactics they'd normally use on a consumer who doesn't know his or her rights will now be useless to them, and they'll be more likely to agree to your terms.

* If you have accounts that you KNOW are going to go into default, don't wait; call your creditors now to negotiate a deal. Be proactive and start negotiating at the first sign of trouble. See David's Real Life Success Story in Chapter 15. Keep records of everything to support your case and efforts should you decide to take the final step of filing a lawsuit.

* Get everything in writing. When it comes to agreements with collection agencies or creditors and the terms they agree to on the telephone, words mean NOTHING.

Wait

Chapter 14 explains Statute of Limitations and the 7-Year Reporting Period. There you will find important advice that will help you decide whether you should wait for the derogatory information to fall off of your report, or not. Here's what you need to take into consideration:

- If the statute of limitations has expired on a debt, then you are no longer legally liable to pay that debt. You cannot be sued and your wages cannot be garnished. However, the item can still remain on your credit report for the 7-Year Reporting Period and you may be denied credit due to an open derogatory balance on your credit reports.

- Once the 7-Year Reporting Period runs, you can have that item removed from your credit report altogether. There are exceptions for public records as laid out in Chapter 14; however, when that 7-Year Reporting Period expires you are free and clear.

It's a personal decision. If you are a year from the 7-Year Reporting Period and you cannot afford to pay the debt, then wait it out. However, if you are able to pay the derogatory AND negotiate a deletion, you can arrange to have the item removed earlier and get on with your financial goals.

Step 6: Get Your Mix In Check

I've addressed, at great length, the importance of maintaining open credit card accounts. Even if you have installment accounts (i.e., auto loan, education loan, mortgage), you still need credit card accounts. If you find yourself in a position of needing to add new credit accounts to your credit profile, I advise you to go back and review Chapters 7 and 10. The information in these two chapters will ensure that when you need to add new credit to your mix of credit that you do so in a way that does not detract from your scores.

1. If you don't have credit cards, get them. Chapter 7 outlines the do's and don'ts of applying for and using credit cards.

2. Opt out of receiving promotional credit offers. Now you know that quality credit is essential to maintaining high credit scores. Opting out of receiving misleading pre-approved offers will not only

protect you from receiving unauthorized hard inquiries, but it will also prevent you from applying for low quality, high costing credit desperately or unnecessarily. You can opt out by calling 1(888)5-OPTOUT, 1(888)567-8688.

3. Try to have at least two active major credit card accounts.

4. An installment account will really help the mix of credit. If you need to make a major purchase, don't pay cash. A co-signed installment loan is a much better option than paying cash for a car or other item.

5. Don't close credit card accounts at all, with the following exceptions: closing a joint account after a divorce; removing your name from an authorized user account that has incurred negative history or has high balance-to-limit ratios; or in the case of identity theft.

6. Don't pay off installment loans. It does not help improve your credit scores. The scoring system wants to see that you can follow a payment agreement over a certain period of time (i.e. $250.00 per month for a period of 5 years with no late pays).

Step 7: Manage Your Debt Strategically

When I create a credit improvement strategy for my clients, the first thing I do is analyze their open credit accounts. I do so because this is where the real meat of the score is; three of the five factors that make up your credit scores are directly related to open credit: Amounts Owed; Mix of Credit; and Length of Credit History. That's 55% of your credit score, or 467.5 points.

As I have explained in this book, there's no way around having open credit. But that's just the most basic element of open credit. Once you have the open credit, you have to manage it strategically so that you can increase your scores. This is your strongest tool for gaining access to credit score points in the shortest period of time. Review Chapters 7 and 8 for details on how to avoid mistakes that can undermine your take action plan.

To stay on top of your open accounts, you need to have all of your account information in one place. This way you can manage and maintain your accounts every month. A spreadsheet will enable you to instantly access your payment information and will be a quick reference to make sure your balance-to-limit ratios are in check. You can create your own spreadsheet, or you can download my 10-Step TAP Worksheet at http://www.lindaferrari.com. At the very least, your spreadsheet should include the following columns:

- Type of Account (i.e. credit card, overdraft, car loan, mortgage)
- Creditor Name & Account #
- Terms
- Open Date
- End Date
- Due Date
- Statement Date
- Balance
- Limit
- Current Ratio (for revolving accounts only)
- 30% Ratio (to give you an idea of where your balance should be if you want to improve your credit scores)
- 50% (to give you an idea of where your balance should be if you want to maintain your credit scores)

Here are some important reminders:

1. Stay current on all open accounts. Remember, one late pay will drop your score by 80 points. So, if you gain points from removing negative history, one mistake like this in your open credit can wipe out the effectiveness of your plan and goal.

2. When you are looking to improve your credit scores, make sure that revolving account balances stay below 30% of their limit at all times. As a general rule, make sure that they stay below 50% of limit if you are looking to maintain the scores that you have.

3. Make sure that your open positive accounts are reporting to all three bureaus.

4. Make sure that all credit card limits and balances are reporting accurately.

5. Immediately remove authorized user accounts if there is negative history or high balances reported on that account. Even if an authorized user account is your only revolving account, if there is negative history or a high balance, it will keep your scores down. Get it removed and apply for your own secured credit card.

   Do not assume that joint accounts are joint accounts. Especially if there is negative history on that account. Call to confirm whether or not you are a joint owner or authorized user.

Step 8: Disputing Do's & Don'ts

Throughout this book I have given you a lot of advice to help you avoid mistakes and not waste unnecessary time or money. I've shown you how to manage open credit accounts and how to optimally use credit.

In the world of disputing credit, there are also many mistakes that consumers make daily that not only cause their credit scores to go down but that can also cause them to lose a valid challenge with the credit bureaus. Here are some tips that will help you avoid making the most common credit disputing mistakes:

1. **Dispute to the credit bureaus first.** I always advise my clients to first dispute derogatory accounts with the credit bureaus before pursing more in-depth solutions. This way, any items that don't belong on the report will be removed. Doing so will save you a lot of time in pursing dispute activity with collection agencies or creditors who 1) don't exist anymore, or 2) don't have your records on file anymore.

2. **Not all creditors report to all three credit bureaus**. One of the most important pieces of advice I can give you when it comes to disputing derogatory accounts is to make sure that you ONLY dispute with the credit bureaus that are reporting the derogatory item. Remember, not all creditors report to all three credit bureaus, so if you send a letter of dispute to a bureau that is not reporting a negative item, you risk having that item added to that bureau report.

> ### WORD OF CAUTION
>
> In an effort to minimize costs, many credit repair companies make the mistake of sending blanket dispute letters to all three credit bureaus. If you are going to work with a credit repair company, you must make sure that they start your dispute process with reports from all three credit bureaus.

3. **Send Certified.** If finances will allow, try to send all correspondence certified. In my experience, when the credit bureaus receive correspondence certified they take disputes seriously and are more likely to pay attention and respond more quickly.

   There is no need to pay additional fees for a registered return receipt. All you need to have is proof that they received your letter, and you can print off a certified tracking receipt from the post office website the day after delivery.

4. **Refer to dispute identifiers.** The dispute identifier is a number assigned to a credit report by the credit bureau for identification purposes and for tracking disputes. If you do not refer to the dispute identifier number in response to a credit bureau's investigation results, you risk having to start your dispute process over again. Each bureau labels its dispute identifier numbers differently, as follows:

   • Equifax – Confirmation No.

   • Experian – File No.

   • TransUnion – Report No.

5. **Avoid being labeled "Frivolous."** Inundating credit bureaus with dispute letters is the worst strategy you can use. Under Section 611 of the Fair Credit Reporting Act, a credit bureau has the right to consider your disputes frivolous or irrelevant. If you inundate the bureaus with letters that do not have supporting documents, the bureaus will eventually refuse to reinvestigate. Here is the language:

   (3) Determination That Dispute Is Frivolous or Irrelevant

   A) *In general.* Notwithstanding paragraph (1), a

consumer reporting agency may terminate a reinvestigation of information disputed by a consumer under that paragraph if the agency reasonably determines that the dispute by the consumer is frivolous or irrelevant, including by reason of a failure by a consumer to provide sufficient information to investigate the disputed information.

Here are some tips to help you avoid being labeled as *frivolous*:

- Don't dispute more than 2-3 items per letter, with the exception of wrong names (aka's), wrong addresses, employment information, and bankruptcy re-list items (accounts that should be included in a bankruptcy).

- First, dispute items for which you have documented proof. These items should be disputed on individual letters. Once you receive confirmation from the credit bureaus that they have corrected the reporting on these accounts, then you can move onto the next level of disputing items for which you lack proof.

- If there are multiple credit items that you are disputing, you should not waste your time or risk reaching this dispute threshold for late pays that are over 24 months old, unless you have documented proof to support your claim.

- Each credit bureau has several different addresses. You can find a list of these addresses on my site at http://www. lindaferrari.com. I recommend that my clients dispute to the various addresses with different items. This way, they remove the risk of having their re-dispute letters end up in the hands of the person who denied their claim in the first place, and this also allows them to dispute more than 2-3 items at a time.

6. **Send proof of social security and proof of current address** with every letter that you send to the credit bureaus.

7. **Don't dispute items together with someone else–EVER.** For instance, if you and your spouse are both disputing items on your credit reports, you MUST dispute separately; otherwise

you run a risk of having the credit bureaus cross over the data (good and bad) on your files. This would create months of work in getting those items removed after the fact.

8. **Never send originals of documents** that support your claim (such as a note marked "paid" or a canceled check); send only copies and keep the originals.

9. **Be realistic, don't give up. Follow-through.** Stay the course. If you walk 50 miles, you have to come back—50 miles—and although this book gives you the tools to help you get back faster, know that long-lasting credit improvement takes time.

Step 9: What If You Don't Have Credit?

If you do not have a credit history, then it's time to start building one. But the question is, how do you get credit if you don't have credit? Here are some great tips:

- **Start Small.** If you do not have credit, lenders and banks will look to other factors that can help them decide if you are a credit risk or not. Here are the areas that can help you get their attention:

    a) **Open a checking and savings account at a major bank.** When you have active bank accounts in good standing, you are creating a history of being able to manage money. I advise starting with a major bank for two reasons: 1) After establishing a relationship with the bank, you will want to apply for a credit card or small installment loan. Major banks are more apt to offer special programs for consumers who are trying to establish or rebuild credit; and 2) Major banks report to all three credit bureaus usually every 30 days, which is what you will need to establish credit quickly.

    b) **Pay your rent and utilities on time.** If you do not have established credit, you are not completely out of luck. Some lenders will pull a report that will show them whether or not consumers pay their rent and utility bills on time. If they like what they see, they may approve you for credit.

That is why it is extremely important to pay these day-to-day living expenses on time.

c) **Show stability in your employment**. Your ability to hold a steady job will improve the likelihood of being approved for credit.

- **Open a Credit Card Account.** If you are just starting out, I would suggest having two major credit cards. Chapters 7 and 10 outline the do's and don'ts of applying for and using credit cards. Be sure to review these chapters prior to going out and applying for a credit card.

- **Talk to your bank.** Banks, especially during and after a nationwide credit crisis, offer many programs to help their clients build and re-establish credit in the form of revolving and small installment accounts. Go into your bank and speak to a representative directly about your options. Make sure that you are very clear on costs, future adjustments and, of course, interest rates—especially universal default rate (see Chapter 8).

- **Join a Credit Union.** A credit union is more willing to consider items other than existing credit accounts when reviewing your application for a credit card or loan, such as your personal and financial information. This makes getting the loan much easier. As outlined above, if you demonstrate your stability by making regular deposits to your credit union accounts, paying your rent and utility bills on time, a credit union is a good option.

- **Be Selective.** As discussed in Chapters 7 and 10, apply only for credit that you know is considered high quality, and credit that reports to the three major credit bureaus (you can find out by calling the creditor and asking which credit bureaus they report to); otherwise there will be no proof of your payment patterns and you will add unwanted inquiries, which lowers your credit scores.

- **Keep inquiries to a minimum.** Only apply for accounts that you have a chance of getting. This means avoid applying for platinum cards that you know you don't qualify for, and avoid pre-approved credit card offers that you receive in the mail. Too many inquiries will hurt your credit and your credit scores. (See Chapter 11)

• **Become An Authorized User On A Family Member's or Spouse's Account.** With the new guidelines from FICO as outlined in the new Fair and Accurate Credit Transaction Act, there is much controversy about whether or not authorized user accounts still help establish credit, and my experience proves that they do if you carry the same last name as the credit card owner.

My advice is to build your *own* credit, if possible, because that gives you power and control; however, as a last resort this option will help. To maximize the benefit of this option, make sure that the account you are being added to belongs to someone you trust, who has NO negative history reporting at all, who has and keeps a balance under 30% of the limit, and finally, whose account is at least 2-3 years old.

It will take 4-6 months before you will begin seeing your credit in the form of reports or credit scores, so it's important—in the meantime—that you keep your new accounts current. Just because new accounts don't show up on a credit report for new credit users, it doesn't mean that you will not suffer a severe score penalty if you pay late.

If you are starting fresh, you are lucky because you have a clean slate and you have this book.

Step 10: Commit To A Maintenance Plan

Everything we do in life revolves around maintenance. We maintain our cars, our homes, and our yards. We maintain our teeth, our appliances, our investment portfolios, and our health. The same diligence should apply to maintaining your credit. To implement strong credit scores for life, you must initiate and adhere to a solid maintenance plan.

The following tips make it easy for you to start strong and stay strong and see your plan through from initial fixes to long-term maintenance that will help you achieve long-term financial health.

1. **Join an online credit watch program.** A credit watch program will give you continued access to your credit reports and scores, and will also notify you when there is any activity—normal or un-

usual—on your credit reports with all three credit bureaus. There are two reasons to sign up for a credit watch program:

a) When you set out on a take action plan, you need to commit to seeing it through. This is the most difficult part of the credit improvement process. My experience in working with thousands of clients has proven over and over again that once they begin their action plan, the *not knowing* and *waiting* part can be very unsettling. Many consumers either pay a fortune to pull their credit reports every 30-45 days or they mistakenly have their credit report pulled several times by lenders because they want to know exactly where they stand. Unfortunately, doing this causes hard inquiries (see Chapter 11), which can bring a consumer's credit scores down by several points. By signing up for an online credit watch program you keep the cost to a minimum, you don't hurt your scores, and you have access to your information all the time.

b) The second reason to sign up for a credit watch program is as follows: Most people are extremely busy, or they simply cannot stick with a plan. Think about it, if gyms actually had to provide services to everyone who signed up for membership, those services would be so delayed that most people would either complain and ask for their money back, or just go to a more elite club that is not oversold. The reality is that most people who sign up for membership, don't go. It's the same with credit. Everyone starts out with the best of intentions, but quickly become lackadaisical after the big points have been regained. However, credit management for life requires a commitment to credit maintenance.

If you are going to make the investment, here's what you should look for in a program:

- Access to updated credit reports and credit scores for ALL three credit bureaus every 30 days.

- DAILY monitoring of your credit notifying you

269

if someone tries to access your credit for any reason.

- Notification of any changes in your credit profile or score.

- Identity theft insurance.

The cost of a credit watch program can vary anywhere from $80 to $150 per year. Usually, most offer a trial period for 30 to 60 days for a minimal fee. If you are not happy with the service, be sure to cancel your membership before the trial period ends.

2. **Order your credit reports from the three major bureaus directly every 6-12 months.** Per Chapter 5, online credit reports and credit watch companies are great for monthly maintenance; however, these reports do not provide the full picture. For this reason, in addition to joining a credit watch program, I advise my clients to pull their credit reports from the three credit bureaus directly as follows:

- If they are active with their credit, I have them check their data at the bureau level every 6 months.

- If they are not applying for credit and have not received any notifications of unusual activity on their credit watch accounts, then I have them check their data at the bureau level once a year.

This is when you want to look for variations in personal identification and demographic information, accounts that don't belong to you, check credit card limits, and open/close status. This is the time to give your credit an annual physical.

3. **Take responsibility for keeping records and proof documents.** If there is one thing you've learned by reading this book, it is that in our scoring system, consumers are guilty until they can prove themselves innocent. The story doesn't matter, and getting an item updated or removed without proof can take months or even years. This is why keeping records, files, proof of payments and creditor agreements is extremely important to maintaining strong credit.

You now know that it takes only one inaccurate item to drop scores by up to 100 points. If you stay organized with your paperwork, then you can eliminate months of wasted time and frustration in getting those items corrected. Here are some tips:

a) **Keep copies of past credit reports.** You should try to keep a copy of your credit report from the three credit bureaus on file (electronically or physically) for the past seven years. Frequently clients tell me that a derogatory account is older than the current credit report shows. New collections are re-dated all the time—which will also re-date the debt. When this occurs, an older copy of the report may indicate: 1) when the item was actually charged off, which would help verify the real date of last delinquency on the account; and 2) prove that the account has been re-dated.

   This is why retaining a copy of an older credit report is extremely useful in proving your case. It can verify the statute of limitations and confirm whether or not the 7-Year Reporting Period has actually expired.

b) **Create a file system for online bill payments.** Online bill payments are very convenient. They also require a good deal of trust. When consumers make their bill payments online, there is no guarantee that the creditor will record the payment on time. For this reason, it's important that you develop a system to keep track of online receipts. I advise my clients to take a screenshot of their payment confirmation pages and email it to themselves. Once they receive those emails, they should create a folder in Outlook, or another email program, dedicated to that one creditor. The subject line of the email should be the Creditor Name and Month of Payment.

c) **Keep a spreadsheet of your open credit accounts.** One of the most common responses I get from a prospective client who has late pays is that he or she "thought" the bill had been paid on time. Then, when asked to track the payment information, all of a sudden it becomes an overwhelming process to contact the bank, look for the cleared checks, and confirm the date the payment was made and what month it was for. Having your open credit account and creditor contact information in one place makes it much easier to be sure you are on top of your payments so that not even one late pay occurs due to oversight. It's also a great way to make sure that your debt to ratio levels on your revolving accounts are in check. You can either add a custom report to your existing accounting software (i.e., QuickBooks or Quicken), or you can create a separate spreadsheet as outlined in Step 7 of this TAP. Whichever is easier for you. You can also access my 10-Step TAP worksheet on my site at http://www.lindaferrari.com to help you get started.

THE REAL DEAL

If your doctor tells you that you now must take heart medication every day for the rest of your life or you will die prematurely, you would follow those orders, wouldn't you? And, you would find a way to adhere to that plan so you can live a longer, healthier life, and be there for those who matter most to you. Trust me when I tell you that this same type of commitment is required for you to maintain credit management for life, to ensure that your Take Action Plan is a "Take Control of the Rest of Your Life Plan." While credit management is not a matter of life or death, it is certainly a matter of long-term servitude vs. long-term happiness that is found in financial freedom. When it comes to your health, you would make sure that no matter what it takes, no matter what the cost, you will do everything that you can to live longer. Why not make sure that you put that same effort into your financial future? Of course you would if you had the tools—and now you do.

This book, the culmination of my professional experience, includes in one valuable resource, all of the critical information that you need to improve your credit scores and your financial outlook, for now and forever.

This valuable information will help to ensure a brighter financial future for you and your family. You'll be able to get the credit you need to live the life you want to live. Higher credit scores will open doors for you to spend less for the mortgages, car payments and credit card interest rates, and will help you save more for your retirement.

I hope I have left you with a lasting understanding of the significance of good credit and the many benefits you can enjoy by simply monitoring your own credit history and taking a proactive position when it comes to your most important number.

I hope that you share my enthusiasm for the financial future you can achieve by understanding and implementing the steps that make such a big difference in your life. I hope I have left you with an understanding and an enthusiasm for what you can achieve by simply getting started. Finally, I hope this book has left an indelible mark on you to go out and make your life better—to achieve THE BIG SCORE.

A Personal Note From Linda

I always knew that my calling was to help people. Whether I would become a doctor, a nurse, or a teacher, I knew I had to stay true to my vision and always keep the faith that one day the answer would be clear.

Like everyone else, I have done many things in my life—from being an executive for a major Hollywood studio, to working for a non-profit promoting better economic conditions for less fortunate countries. It's a long story of how I became involved in credit improvement and education, but the good news for you and me and millions of people across this nation is that I did. Once I stepped in, there was no turning back for me, regardless of how difficult times got.

The rewards from day one were abundant, and I don't mean financial. I mean, instead, the appreciation and gratitude I've received from the thousands of individuals I have helped. I have stories that will make you cry and make you laugh. Stories about receiving soiled paperwork in the mail from clients who have just lost everything to a hurricane or flood (including Katrina). But there are two stories that stand out in my mind and my heart that I want to share with you in closing of this book.

BETTY

The first story is about Betty. Betty is a married mom of four wonderful children. When she first called me, our conversation was like every other conversation I have with prospective clients; about her goals, her credit, and payment options. But after hanging up, I knew that there was something more to this woman than a simple desire to improve her credit history. So, completely out of professional character, I picked up the phone and I called her back. She was surprised to hear my voice and by her response I knew that she thought I was calling her back to sell her something.

All I said was, "Betty, is there anything else I need to know about your case that will help me create a successful strategy for you to meet your score goal?" And she said, "Yes, Linda, I was just diagnosed with cancer and if I can't get approved for the refinance soon, my children and my husband may be left without a home."

I was devastated by her admission, and I struggled to maintain my own composure. At the moment, my job had just become so much bigger than helping someone add points to her credit scores. I felt honored to have been the person that Betty, somehow, got connected to. All I wanted to do was get to work.

Mostly due to collections, past and recent, Betty had scores in the high 500s. So we started with the 10-Step TAP, and when we got to Step 5 her focus was strictly on negotiation. With my coaching and oversight, Betty employed all of the techniques in Chapter 14 and 18 to first validate debts, and then to negotiate debts for pennies on the dollar. By the fifth month, her scores had gone up approximately 130 points.

Betty and I talked frequently while she was in the program. I noticed that she would always call me either from or right after treatment. I guess that's why I remember it so clearly. We'd talk about how she was doing, about her kids, her husband, and we would always talk about the progress she was making in her credit improvement plan. It would energize her to pull her scores and see that they had gone up again. Her strength and her commitment were remarkable. She stayed true to the course, through it all.

Betty had her final surgery about 6 months after starting her credit improvement program, and that was about 6 months ago. She was approved for her refinance, and her family is now safe and sound, and so is she. The treatment went well, and although she has a long haul in front of her, she is strong and in her own words, not only physically, but financially, because her new improved credit scores have opened up opportunity for her to refinance everything, including her car loans.

JOHN

The next story is about John, 40 years old. John, a husband and a father of two, lived with his in-laws and things were falling apart. His marriage was just about to explode, the in-laws wanted them out, and he was pretty down and out when he got me on the phone.

John explained to me that the worst part of not being able to buy a home was the humiliation of not being able to take care of his family. It wasn't that he couldn't afford it, he just couldn't find a lender to approve him because of his credit scores. His vision of what his life would be was much different than reality, and he felt completely defeated. His credit situation was pretty bad, and we had a lot of work to do.

John's program entailed adding new credit, and cleaning up the old. He had several bankruptcy items that were not included in the bankruptcy, still showing balances and inaccurate dates for when items became delinquent. After using the 10-Step TAP, in 6 months John's scores went from the low 500s into the 680s.

My phone rang, and when I picked it up there was a voice on the other end screaming and cheering. It was John calling to tell me that they had been approved for the loan and were planning to move into their new home within 30 days. John told me that his whole life had changed. His marriage was improved, he felt good again about life and about himself, and the fact that he was preparing to move into his OWN home made him 'over the top' happy. I, too, was 'over the top' happy and full of gratitude for his appreciation.

Two weeks later I called John at home to see how things were going with the move, and his wife answered. She proceeded to tell me that John, on the day he called me, had died of a brain tumor. She said "Thank you," and reminded me that her and the children would be moving into their new home. She said that John was never happier than he was when was approved for his new home loan.

I want to give thanks to all of my clients for their support. Without them, I wouldn't have been able to write this book that I am hoping will help a great many people throughout the world.

These two stories prove that it can be done, under any circumstances. I wish you the best of luck in moving forward in attaining the highest of credit scores, and in changing your life for the better under any condition.

If this book has helped you, I would love to hear from you and to learn how it has changed your life. The email address is testimonials@lindaferrari.com.

Best Regards,

Index

ssory note, 138
notional inquiry, 104
ublic records, 82, 183-185
duplicate reporting, 30

R
race, 68, 126, 127
ratio, 73, 74, 77, 84, 110, 272
rebuilding, 167, 180, 266
refinance, 25, 43, 249
reinvestigation, 33-34, 258, 265
religion, 68, 126, 127
renegotiate, 156
renewing
  7-year reporting period, 143
  business license, 46
  date of last delinquency, 139
  judgments, 138
  statute of limitations, 139, 198
  student loans, 187
renting
  a car, 46, 47
  a home, 47
  an apartment, 47
  credit reporting, 266
repossessions, 186
  foreclosure, 216
revolving accounts, 71-80
  balances, 76, 77, 100
  home equity line of credit, 98
  keeping a balance, 110
  mix of credit, 98
  reporting, 54
  statement date, 77
  statute of limitations, 138
rights
  Consumer Credit Reporting Act of
    1968, 121
  Credit Repair Organizations Act
    (CROA), 134
  Equal Credit Opportunity Act

(ECOA), 126
Fair and Accurate Credit Transac-
  tion Act (FACTA), 125
Fair Credit Billing Act (FCBA),
  129
Fair Credit Reporting Act (FCRA),
  122
Fair Debt Collection Practices Act
  (FDCPA), 131
Health Insurance Portability And
  Accountability Act of 1996
  (HIPAA), 135
suing, 117, 120
U.S. Code, 121
violation of ,85, 96, 124, 135, 194,
  205, 206, 215

S
salary, 69, 115
savings account, 98, 188, 266
secret formula, 26
secured credit card, 74
  bankruptcy, 181
  mix of credit, 98
security deposit, 47
settlement, 159-160, 186, 219, 220
sex, 68, 127, 128
short sale, 219-220
small claims, 208
Social Security Number
  disputing, 258, 265
  errors, 94
  identity theft, 235-241
  length of history, 95
  no score reporting, 66
soft inquiry, 103
software, credit scoring, 52-62
statement date, 76, 77, 79
Statute of Limitations, 138-140
  judgments, 138
  open-ended accounts (credit cards),